Organizational Outsourcing Readiness

Empirically Investigating the Role of Client's IT Capability, Knowledge, and Alignment for Outsourcing Success

Sebastian F. Martin

Sebastian F. Martin

ORGANIZATIONAL OUTSOURCING READINESS

Empirically Investigating the Role of Client's IT Capability,
Knowledge, and Alignment for Outsourcing Success

ibidem-Verlag
Stuttgart

Bibliografische Information der Deutschen Nationalbibliothek
Die Deutsche Nationalbibliothek verzeichnet diese Publikation in der Deutschen Nationalbibliografie; detaillierte bibliografische Daten sind im Internet über http://dnb.d-nb.de abrufbar.

Bibliographic information published by the Deutsche Nationalbibliothek
Die Deutsche Nationalbibliothek lists this publication in the Deutsche Nationalbibliografie; detailed bibliographic data are available in the Internet at http://dnb.d-nb.de.

Coverabbildung: © Chris / PIXELIO

Dissertation, Fachbereich Wirtschaftswissenschaften, Goethe-Universität Frankfurt

∞

Gedruckt auf alterungsbeständigem, säurefreien Papier
Printed on acid-free paper

ISBN-10: 3-8382-0029-2
ISBN-13: 978-3-8382-0029-3

© *ibidem*-Verlag
Stuttgart 2010

Alle Rechte vorbehalten

Das Werk einschließlich aller seiner Teile ist urheberrechtlich geschützt. Jede Verwertung außerhalb der engen Grenzen des Urheberrechtsgesetzes ist ohne Zustimmung des Verlages unzulässig und strafbar. Dies gilt insbesondere für Vervielfältigungen, Übersetzungen, Mikroverfilmungen und elektronische Speicherformen sowie die Einspeicherung und Verarbeitung in elektronischen Systemen.

All rights reserved. No part of this publication may be reproduced, stored in or introduced into a retrieval system, or transmitted, in any form, or by any means (electronic, mechanical, photocopying, recording or otherwise) without the prior written permission of the publisher. Any person who does any unauthorized act in relation to this publication may be liable to criminal prosecution and civil claims for damages.

Printed in Germany

Acknowledgements

This work originates from a project of the E-Finance Lab at the House of Finance, Goethe University, Frankfurt. I would like to express my gratitude to the people who have supported me through the course of this research, hereby contributing to its quality and success.

First and foremost, I would like to thank my academic advisor, Prof. Dr. Wolfgang König, for offering me the chance to work in a creative and inspiring environment such as the E-Finance Lab and for his guidance throughout the dissertation process. Likewise, I am indebted to Prof. Dr. Peter Gomber, who acted as co-referee for my dissertation thesis, to Prof. Dr. Martin Natter for willingly accepting to chair the dissertation committee, and to Prof. Dr. Günter Beck for acting as a member of this committee.

I would also like to thank my dear colleague and friend Dr. Daniel Beimborn, who co-authored most of the articles presented in this book. His kind and patient advice and his continuous support throughout the course of this dissertation were priceless.

Furthermore, I am grateful for the opportunity I've had to work with, and learn from, Prof. Dr. Tim Weitzel and Prof. Dr. Heinz-Theo Wagner. Their positive influence on my development and progress extends beyond the academic domain.

Many thanks go to Dr. Stefan Blumenberg and to Prof. Mihir Parikh, who I worked with in various research projects and who provided me with valuable ideas many times.

Finally, all my love and thankfulness go to my wife Cristina, the driving factor and main source of motivation for me during this academic quest. Without her patience and support, this book would hardly have been possible and words alone cannot adequately express my gratitude. Dear Cristina, I lovingly dedicate this book to you and to our unborn son.

Dr. Sebastian Martin

Table of Contents

Introductory Paper: Organizational Outsourcing Readiness   1
Sebastian F. Martin

Getting Ready for Success: May Alignment Be of Help?   35
Sebastian F. Martin, Daniel Beimborn, Mihir A. Parikh, Tim Weitzel

Organizational Readiness for Business Process Outsourcing: A Model of Determinants and Impact on Outsourcing Success   57
Sebastian F. Martin, Daniel Beimborn, Mihir A. Parikh, Tim Weitzel

IT Capability and Outsourcing Readiness: The Effect of Human, Technical, and Knowledge IT Resources on Outsourcing Success   81
Sebastian F. Martin, Daniel Beimborn, Mihir A. Parikh, Tim Weitzel, Wolfgang König

Process Documentation, Operational Alignment, and Flexibility in IT Outsourcing Relationships: A Knowledge-Based Perspective   123
Sebastian F. Martin, Heinz-Theo Wagner, Daniel Beimborn

The Impact of Alignment on Outsourcing Outcomes: Empirical Evidence from the German Banking Industry   159
Sebastian F. Martin

Introductory Paper:
Organizational Outsourcing Readiness

Sebastian F. Martin
E-Finance Lab
Institute for Information Systems
Goethe University, Frankfurt, Germany
smartin@wiwi.uni-frankfurt.de

Abstract

How can prospective outsourcing clients prepare their internal organizations to meet the challenges associated with the outsourcing venture with little penalty in time, cost, and effort? Along this guiding question, this thesis empirically investigates how three factors from the client's internal organizational context affect the outcomes of outsourcing: the client's IT capability, the available explicit knowledge in form of business process documentation, and the level of alignment between the client's IT and business domains. Based on qualitative and quantitative empirical data, each of the three client-internal factors is shown to have a significant inter-organizational impact, affecting the quality of the relationship between client and provider, the vendor's performance, and outsourcing success.

1 Introduction

1.1 Motivation and Objective of the Thesis

A mature research strand on outsourcing has evolved during the past 15 years, covering a wide range of questions that deal with *why* and *what* to outsource, with contract design, with the management of the ongoing relationship between client and vendor, and with the actual outcomes of outsourcing (Dibbern et al.

2004). From the client's perspective, various determinants of outsourcing success have been identified and analyzed in previous literature, such as the proper degree of outsourcing (i.e., determining the "right" functions to be handed over to an external provider) (Lacity et al. 1996), the selection of adequate outsourcing vendors (McFarlan and Nolan 1995; Michell and Fitzgerald 1997), appropriate contract design (Gellings 2007; Goo et al. 2009), and the quality of the relationship between client and outsourcing provider (Blumenberg 2008; Goles and Chin 2005).

But what is the role of a client's *internal organization* in determining the success or failure of outsourcing? Research addressing the readiness of the client organization as an outsourcing success factor is scarce, although there is indication in literature that it may play an outstanding role for reaching the intended benefits of outsourcing. For example, Ranganathan and Balaji identify outsourcing readiness, which is defined as "a firm's ability to prepare its internal organization to undertake [outsourcing] activities" (Ranganathan and Balaji 2007, p. 150), to be one of ten critical capabilities needed for successfully outsourcing IS work to offshore providers. Ross and Westerman (2004, p.5) note that "the firms' ability to generate value from outsourcing depends on the maturity of their IT architectures" and Barthélemy (2001) suggests that the lack of adequate resources, which affects the client's outsourcing readiness, might translate into costly project breakdowns, significant project delays and even complete project failures. However, these references are largely anecdotal and lack in-depth analyses.

The absence of research focusing on the client firm and its ex ante preparedness for outsourcing, along with numerous preliminary discussions with practitioners from both outsourcing clients and vendors, who suggested that missing outsourcing readiness on the client side often represents a major reason for project failure, determined us to address the following question:

What is the role of a firm's internal organization for the eventual success or failure of an outsourcing venture?

Along this guiding question, this dissertation theoretically underpins and empirically investigates the particular role of three different client-side factors in shaping the relationship with the outsourcing vendor and the outcomes of outsourcing. These three factors represent the different internal domains of the client's organization: (1) client's IT capability, representing the IT domain, (2) the availability of high-quality, explicit knowledge about the client's business processes, representing the business domain, and (3) the operational alignment between client's IT and business people, representing the tying element between the first two domains.

1.2 Structure of the Thesis

This cumulative dissertation consists of a purely theoretical part (conceptual papers 1 and 2) and an empirical one (papers 3, 4, and 5). **Paper 1** theoretically develops the concept of organizational readiness as consisting of a business dimension, which reflects the structural preparedness of the firm to engage into inter-organizational cooperation, and an IT dimension, reflecting the technological preparedness of the firm in terms of IT sophistication and technological know-how. **Paper 2** extends this argument and develops a three-dimensional outsourcing readiness construct by including process readiness, as a special readiness dimension in the context of business process outsourcing (BPO), which refers to the existence of rules, procedures, and clear management practices for the processes affected by BPO. Moreover, both papers discuss the role of IT business alignment in shaping the firm's ability to establish and maintain inter-organizational cooperative linkages with service providers.

The empirical part of this dissertation includes both qualitative and quantitative research results. Based on a series of interviews with managers from client and vendor organizations, **paper 3** provides a detailed view of the IT dimension of organizational readiness, investigating and categorizing the ways by which a client organization's existing IT capability may foster or inhibit successful outsourcing. **Paper 4** draws on quantitative data to address a particular aspect of the business dimension of organizational readiness, namely the role of business process documentation, as a form of explicit knowledge about the client's business domain, in shaping the relationship between client and outsourcing vendor. Finally, **paper 5** brings IT and business dimensions together, analyzing how the operational alignment between people from client's IT and business domains affects the quality of inter-organizational communication between client and outsourcing vendor as well as the service quality provided by the vendor. Each of these articles will be discussed in more detail in chapter 5 of this introductory paper.

1.3 Focus of the Thesis

The focus of the thesis narrows with each paper. The first (conceptual) paper discusses organizational readiness in the context of inter-organizational linkages (IOL). The notion of IOL generically refers to any kind of IT-based inter-organizational cooperation and has captured large academic attention since the outset of business-to-business electronic commerce, facilitated by the emergence of the internet and the development of powerful inter-organizational systems and technologies like EDI and XML. This wide focus of the first paper allows us to position organizational readiness as a concept which is applicable to a wide range of inter-organizational cooperation forms (e.g., outsourcing relationships or client-supplier relationships along the industry supply chain) and sets the stage for future research. In the further course of this dissertation, we chose to focus on *outsourcing relationships* as a particular form of inter-organizational cooperation whose outcomes may be decisively affected by the client's readiness.

Consequently, the second (conceptual) paper discusses organizational readiness in the context of *BPO*. BPO represents the broadest-possible form of outsourcing, referring to the externalization of an entire business function, which includes the underlying IT (Fröschl 1999; Gewald and Franke 2007; Lancellotti et al. 2003; Rouse and Corbitt 2004).

The focus is then narrowed again within the third (qualitative) paper, which focuses on *IT outsourcing* (ITO), but without specifically referring to a particular form of ITO (e.g., application management outsourcing or IT infrastructure outsourcing).

Focusing on a specific form of ITO becomes necessary in the (quantitative) papers 4 and 5, which both concentrate on *application management outsourcing* (AMO) as a research object. The choice of such a narrow focus in the last two papers has methodological reasons: asking the respondents to refer to the same type of application excludes much of the potential side-effects from uncontrolled variables that might occur in a wider frameset, allowing for more reliable results. The following figure illustrates the narrowing focus of the thesis.

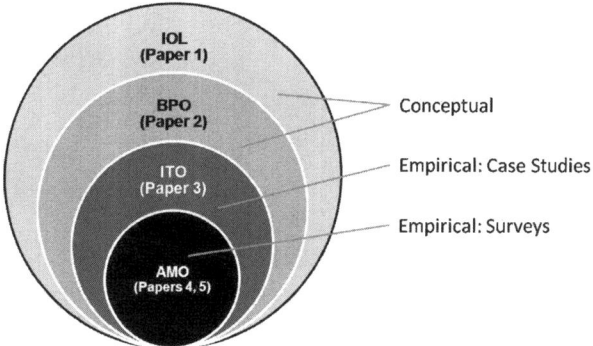

Figure 1: Focus of the Thesis

2 Research Context: The German Financial Industry

Focusing the unit of analysis of empirical research on a single industry is recommended by scholars as a way to cope with the bias that might otherwise occur if research focuses on diverse research contexts (Chiasson and Davidson

2005; Hirschheim 2003). The banking industry was chosen as a research domain for several reasons.

- First, the financial services industry is currently in the midst of a radical transformation process, caused by an ever-increasing competition and supported by the availability of mature and powerful B2B information systems which provide the technical means for automated cooperation across organizational borders. Through its Circular 11/2001, the Federal Financial Supervisory Authority, BaFin, has created the regulatory framework for outsourcing banking activities to third party providers (BaFin 2001). Since then, banks have been increasingly outsourcing not just their IT function, but also entire business processes to specialized service providers. This strong and long-lasting trend towards outsourcing activities, which is expected to grow continuously in the next years (Kraus 2008), makes the financial services industry an ideal domain for the study of client-side outsourcing success factors.

- Second, the banking industry is one of the most highly regulated industry domains worldwide. The strict regulatory guidelines allow for a common reference framework which excludes interfering variables that might otherwise dilute the results if research was to be carried out in a different, less regulated industry. The guidelines from the Basel Committee on Banking stipulate that banks have to make sure that they remain in charge of their own business and in control of their business risks even if a business function or its underlying IT is being outsourced (BIS 2005).

- Third, banks employ especially IT-intensive business processes, since IT represents, besides people, their only production resource. Therefore, a functioning IT is of exorbitant importance for the bank, and the success or failure of an outsourcing venture may decide over its survival on the market.

3 Theoretical Foundation

3.1 Resource-based View

3.1.1 Basics

The Resource-Based View (RBV) (Penrose 1959; Wernerfelt 1984) conceptualizes the firm as a collection of productive resources which are bundled together in an administrative entity. Its basic assumption is that firms are heterogeneous in terms of the resources they possess, and that these differences can explain differences in success and market position (Barney 1991). Competitive advantage and the growth of a firm depend on the ability of the firm to exploit its available resources. "Resources are defined as those tangible (or intangible) assets that are tied semipermanently to the firm" (Spanos and Lioukas 2001, p. 909). Barney (Barney 1991) differentiates between three different types of resources a firm might own or control: physical capital (e.g., equipment, raw materials), human capital (e.g., management team), and organizational capital (e.g., reputation, firm culture). The same resources may be used to render many different services (Penrose 1959). They form the building blocks for a firm's *capabilities*, which represent units of business functionality, defined by Barney as „the ability of firms to use their resources to generate competitive advantages" (Barney 2001, p. 647).

3.1.2 Implications for Outsourcing Readiness

Outsourcing research often builds on the RBV as a theoretical foundation. Especially works dealing with the questions *whether* and *what* to outsource draw on the RBV as a common theoretical framework. For example, the *lack* of competitive internal resources and capabilities has been found in numerous empirical studies to be a main driving factor for the outsourcing decision (Dibbern et al. 2004). A common theoretical viewpoint is that by outsourcing certain functions, firms may profit from the presumed superior competence of specialized service providers.

RBV posits that organizations differ from each other and are able to reach competitive advantage by means of the differences in their resources and capabilities. The implication for organizational outsourcing readiness research is that different organizations must therefore also face differences in their outsourcing readiness – in terms of how well-prepared their internal resources and capabilities are to support outsourcing. Thus, possessing adequate resources and capabilities can confer a competitive advantage to an organization by enabling it to perform outsourcing with fewer penalties in time, costs, and effort as compared to other organizations. While this dissertation builds on this fundamental assumption, the question that consequently arises is *which* resources and capabilities are relevant for successful outsourcing and *what role* do they play for conferring a superior state of outsourcing readiness to an organization. As stated in the introduction, three different client-internal resources and capabilities are empirically analyzed with regard to their impact on the outcomes of outsourcing.

3.2 Knowledge-based View

3.2.1 Basics

Originating from the RBV, the Knowledge-based View (KBV) (Grant 1996) considers knowledge to be the most important resource of the firm and regards knowledge integration, spanning a broad range of knowledge domains, to be the main mechanism for achieving and sustaining competitive advantage (Kogut and Zander 1992). This perspective of 'knowledge as a resource' distinguishes between tacit and explicit knowledge (Nonaka 1994). *Explicit* knowledge refers to knowledge that exists in symbolic or written form (Alavi and Leidner 2001). This kind of knowledge is characterized by ease of communication and transportability across individuals and organizations (Nonaka 1994). In contrast, *tacit* knowledge is bound to individuals and is very difficult or even impossible to articulate and codify and is therefore difficult to transfer. This kind of knowledge is "rooted in action, experience, and involvement in a specific context" (Alavi and Leidner 2001, p.110) and may be learned only through observation and doing. The codifiable part of tacit knowledge has been referred to as *implicit* knowledge and is defined as "knowledge that can be expressed in verbal, symbolic, or written form, but has not yet been expressed" (Lee 2001, p.324). This aspect is especially important in an outsourcing context, because much of the implicit knowledge kept within the heads of the client's employees needs to be made explicit and transferred to the IT outsourcing provider, as we will discuss in the following section.

3.2.2 Implications for Outsourcing Readiness

An important aspect, which needs to be considered when analyzing outsourcing relationships, is that in order to be able to deliver prompt and effective services, the provider firm needs to acquire a thorough understanding of its client's business processes and IT landscape (Dibbern et al. 2008; Tiwana 2003). Successful outsourcing relationships therefore require extensive exchange of knowledge between client and provider (Dibbern et al. 2008; Tiwana 2003), which includes the transfer of knowledge about the client's business processes, IT landscape, organizational structures, communication channels, etc. (Dibbern et al. 2008). Prior literature has acknowledged that knowledge transfer depends on "how easily that knowledge can be transported, interpreted, and absorbed" (Simonin 1999, p.597). However, transferring knowledge is only possible if the client makes the necessary knowledge *available* to the provider. Hence, the client is confronted with the need to internally coordinate various stakeholders from business and IT domains in order to aggregate dispersed information, to consolidate it, and to prepare it for transfer to the provider. Thus, from a knowledge-based perspective, readiness research needs to address and identify factors that foster the client's *ability to internally prepare relevant information*, to make implicit knowledge explicit, and to deliver it to the outsourcing provider.

4 Empirical Research Approach

Since the propositions from the conceptual papers as well as the hypotheses discussed in each of the empirical papers were based on prior literature, the research methodology applied within this dissertation follows the positivist paradigm. However, within this paradigm, some of the research questions pursued and discussed in the empirical papers called for a qualitative research approach, while others called for quantitative research methods. In the following, both research approaches will be discussed separately.

4.1 Qualitative Research

The research question discussed within paper 3 is a typical *"how"*-question in the nomenclature of Yin (2003) (namely, *how* client's existing IT resources affect the successful preparation, implementation, and maintenance of an IT outsourcing relationship). According to Yin (2003), effectively pursuing this kind of question requires a qualitative approach, which, given the fact that the paper analyzes previously hypothesized links, is explanatory in nature.

The case studies discussed in this paper were performed with three different organizations from the financial services industry. In a first step, a series of interviews with eight senior managers from a large German IT service provider was carried out. Multiple rounds of discussions with each of the case study participants were complemented by email exchange and clarifying phone conversations, when needed. As a second step, two antagonistic case studies with German banks were performed, aiming to validate the results obtained from the provider interviews by incorporating the client perspective. One of the two banks had recently completed an outsourcing project, which was considered to be successful because all intended objectives of outsourcing were fully met. The second client case investigated the story of an outsourcing project which, after two years of struggling, had to be aborted and thus was considered by management to be a complete failure.

Throughout the study, rigor was ensured by following the guidelines given by case study methodologists (Dubé and Paré 2003; Eisenhardt 1989; Shanks and Parr 2003; Yin 2003) as outlined below. Data collection was performed systematically, with a clear research focus and a pre-defined research question – which underlines the explanatory character of this qualitative approach.

Construct validity "concerns the issue of whether empirical data in multiple situations leads to the same conclusions, and is improved by multiple sources of evidence" and requires "having key informants review the case study report" (Shanks and Parr 2003, p. 6). This was ensured by addressing senior managers within each firm, who were likely to have a thorough overview over the discussed cases, and by asking them to review the results of the interviews and to confirm their validity. Further evidence like process documentation and excerpts from the firm intranets were also handed over to us by some of our interview partners.

We also accounted for *external validity*, which refers to the generalizability of the qualitative findings, by choosing case study participants with extensive experience in the outsourcing domain and by designing the qualitative study as a two-staged approach. This way, the findings from the provider side could be validated in different settings by comparing them with findings from two antagonistic case studies performed with client organizations.

Internal validity, which is concerned with establishing a causal relationship between the theoretical concepts used in the study and the evidence from the case study data, was ensured by comparing predication from the literature with the evidence from the three different case studies (so-called "pattern matching" (Yin 2003)).

Finally, the *reliability* of the results "concerns the stability and consistency of the study" (Shanks and Parr 2003, p. 6) across different researchers and time. In order to achieve reliable results, case study methodologists suggest using case study databases and the development of a clear case study protocol (Yin 2003). To ensure reliability, we used MaxQDA (version 2), which is a software especially designed for conducting qualitative research. This software allows researchers to store and codify interview transcripts and offers multiple opportunities for case analysis and comparison. Furthermore, a case study protocol was jointly produced by the research team.

4.2 Quantitative Research

4.2.1 Structural Equation Modeling Approaches

In contrast to paper 3, the research questions discussed within **paper 4** (*"What is the impact of business process documentation on outsourcing relationships?"*) and **paper 5** (*"What is the impact of alignment on outsourcing relationships?"*) call for a quantitative research approach, which allows measuring the strength of the respective impact and testing on statistical inference. In both papers, the research models were operationalized as Structural Equation Models (SEM) and were validated using the Partial Least Squares (PLS) statistical technique.

SEMs allow for modeling constructs as latent (i.e., not directly observable) variables, which may be measured by using multiple directly observable indicators or manifest variables (Chin 1998). A rigorous, simultaneous statistical examination of both the strength of theoretical relationships between latent variables and the accuracy of the measures of these variables becomes possible. This has led to SEMs becoming highly popular among social scientists (Qureshi and Compeau 2009).

Different statistical methods are available for the estimation of SEMs. These techniques may be either covariance-based (provided by tools like AMOS and LISREL) or component-based (e.g., PLS). In papers 4 and 5, PLS was chosen for two reasons:

(1) Covariance-based methods focus on overall model fit – i.e., on how well the available data fits a well-established, previously-tested theoretical

model. In contrast, PLS focuses on *prediction* and attempts to minimize residual variance of the dependent variables. Therefore, using PLS is more appropriate if the theoretical model has *not* been tested in prior research (Chin 1998; Gopal et al. 1993).

(2) In contrast to covariance-based methods, which require multivariate normality, PLS does not have distributional assumptions regarding the data. Since the data sets used in the two papers predominantly consisted of not normally distributed variables, PLS became the method of choice for model validation (Chin 1998).

Moreover, recent literature comes in support of PLS as the method of choice for detecting and assessing between-group differences – as it is the case with papers 4 and 5 – in conditions of non-normality, particularly for smaller samples and moderate effect sizes (Qureshi and Compeau 2009).

4.2.2 Empirical Surveys

The two quantitative papers of this dissertation (papers 4 and 5) are based on data from two different surveys.

Paper 4 of this dissertation uses data from the survey "Critical Success Factors in Financial Processes" (survey 1), which was carried out in 2005 as a joint research project of Cluster 1 and Cluster 5 of the E-Finance Lab. Survey 1 addressed the Chief Credit Officers from Germany's 1,000 largest banks and focused on IT business alignment and on the adequate deployment of IT resources as determinants of performance for the credit granting processes in banks. From the 136 completed questionnaires (representing a response rate of 13.6%), a number of 104 respondents indicated that their credit processing system – which was the information system that all respondents were asked to refer to when answering the questionnaire – is externally managed and run by an outsourcing provider (compared to 20 banks stating to use an in-house system and 12 respondents who gave no answer). Consequently, this sub-sample of 104 questionnaires was used for the analysis.

Paper 5 is based on the survey "Successful Management of Outsourcing Relationships" (survey 2), carried out in 2008 by researchers from Cluster 1 together with colleagues from the Chair of Information Systems and Services of the Bamberg University. Survey 2 was dedicated entirely to the preparation and management of outsourcing relationships, again targeting managers from Germany's 1,000 largest banks. For each bank in the sample, we identified the manager who was responsible for the bank's relationship with the vendor firm that provided management services for a particular IT application, namely, the application that supports the process of granting and managing mortgage loans. This survey achieved an effective response rate of 16% (160 returned questionnaires), which were used for the analysis.

For both surveys, the questionnaire items were derived from recent scientific literature and have been validated in pre-tests and expert workshops prior to the survey in order to minimize semantic bias.

5 Main Results

5.1 Paper 1[1]: Conceptualizing the Role of Organizational Readiness and Alignment for Successful Inter-organizational Cooperation

Paper 1 conceptualizes the role played by organizational readiness and IT business alignment in the process of adopting inter-organizational relationships (like outsourcing relationships) between two firms. The paper develops and theoretically underpins a process model that illustrates the impact of organizational readiness and alignment on the outcomes of an inter-

---

[1] Martin, S.F., Beimborn, D., Parikh, M., Weitzel, T.: "Getting Ready for Success: May Alignment Be of Help?". In: 13th Americas Conference on Information Systems (AMCIS 2007), Keystone (CO), USA, 2007.

organizational cooperation venture. It postulates that a firm's intention to adopt inter-organizational linkages by means of inter-organizational systems is driven by isomorphic (i.e., internal and external mimetic, coercive, and normative) pressures to adopt such linkages, and by its general organizational readiness. The concept of organizational readiness for inter-organizational linkages developed in this paper consists of two dimensions:

- The business dimension, termed IOR (inter-organizational relationship) readiness, reflecting the structural preparedness of the firm to establish a new inter-organizational cooperation. It implies the adaptation of processes to meet the needs of the new cooperation, the redistribution of authority and responsibilities, etc.

- The IT dimension, termed IOS (inter-organizational systems) readiness, reflects the technological preparedness of the firm in terms of IT sophistication and know how to either adopt new, or adapt an existing IOS in order to technologically support the cooperation.

Thorough alignment between its IT and business domains affects the client's ability to identify opportunities for inter-organizational cooperation with potential business partners and to reap the benefits from the cooperation by enabling the firm to effectively adapt its organizational structure and IT to meet the demands of the new inter-organizational cooperation. The intense interplay between business and IT people within an organization (corresponding to higher levels of alignment), enables the organization to correctly evaluate the fit between a prospective inter-organizational cooperation and the firm's goals, structure, and financial and technological possibilities (i.e. its organizational readiness to engage into that inter-organizational cooperation). As a result, the firm is enabled to implement the necessary changes on structural and IT level more effectively, in order to become ready for a specific cooperation.

5.2 Paper 2[2]: Conceptualizing Drivers and Dimensions of Outsourcing Readiness

While paper 1 develops a process model describing the impact of outsourcing readiness and alignment on outsourcing success, paper 2 takes a cross-sectional view on the two factors readiness and alignment. This paper has a more narrow focus than the first paper, focusing on business process outsourcing (BPO) instead of inter-organizational cooperation in general. This allows for a more pinpointed discussion of the different dimensions of organizational readiness. The paper develops propositions for two research questions: first, *"What are the relevant dimensions of organizational readiness for BPO and what is their impact on BPO success?"* and second, *"What is the impact of IT business alignment on the achievement of organizational readiness for BPO?"*.

Compared to paper 1, a third dimension is added to the notion of organizational readiness for BPO: the process readiness dimension. It refers to the degree of formalization of the processes affected by BPO, as indicated by the existence of rules, procedures, and clear management practices. The paper postulates that process formalization contributes to the successful implementation of BPO by eliminating ambiguities pertaining to the processes affected by BPO, thereby helping to avoid hidden costs and to achieve the anticipated cost savings. With regard to the IT dimension of outsourcing readiness, it is postulated that a flexible IT infrastructure and a thorough business understanding of client's IT managers allow for a more efficient implementation and maintenance of BPO relationships. Regarding the business dimension, it is reasoned that IT competence of business managers enables them to comprehend and cope with

---

[2] Martin, S.F., Beimborn, D., Parikh, M., Weitzel, T.: "Organizational Readiness for Business Process Outsourcing: A Model of Determinants and Impact on Outsourcing Success". In: Hawaii International Conference on System Sciences (HICSS-41), Big Island (HI), USA, 2008.

IT-related challenges posed by BPO more easily and thus to place their business decisions on a more solid basis.

Together with paper 1, this paper forms the foundation for the subsequent empirical investigation of the impact of client's internal business and IT domains on the process and the eventual outcomes of outsourcing.

5.3 Paper 3[3]: Qualitative Results: How Client's IT Capability Affects Outsourcing Success

Following the preceding conceptualization of outsourcing readiness as consisting of an IT and a business dimension, paper 3 represents the empirical in-depth exploration of the IT dimension's impact on outsourcing success.

The starting premise of this paper is that firms exhibiting superior IT capabilities through their IT resources will experience fewer and lower barriers to successful IT outsourcing. Its aim is to investigate the ways by which an organization's existing IT resources may impact the success of IT outsourcing relationships. The IT dimension is split into three critical IT resources available to a firm, based on the classification of IT resources by Bharadwaj (2000):

- *Human IT resources* refer to the technical and managerial competence of IT personnel in the client firm.

- *Technical IT resources* refer to the state of the technological infrastructure and information systems in the client firm.

- *Knowledge IT resources* refer to the explicitness of firm-specific IT knowledge in form of documentation (e.g., source code, process

---

[3] Martin, S.F., Beimborn, D., Parikh, M., Weitzel, T., König, W.: "IT Capability and Outsourcing Readiness: The Effect of Human, Technical, and Knowledge IT Resources on Outsourcing Success". Submitted for publication to Information & Management.

documentation, statistics about usage, errors, and systems performance, peak times, etc.).

Moreover, these three IT resources are split into several sub-dimensions, according to prior literature. The paper identifies and analyzes the role played by each of these sub-dimensions during the course of the outsourcing process, which is divided into three distinct phases for a more pinpointed examination. The three phases of the outsourcing process are: the *preparation* phase (preparation of the outsourcing deal), the transition phase (implementation of the outsourcing deal), and the ongoing maintenance of the outsourcing relationship. Figure 2 visualizes the research model of paper 3.

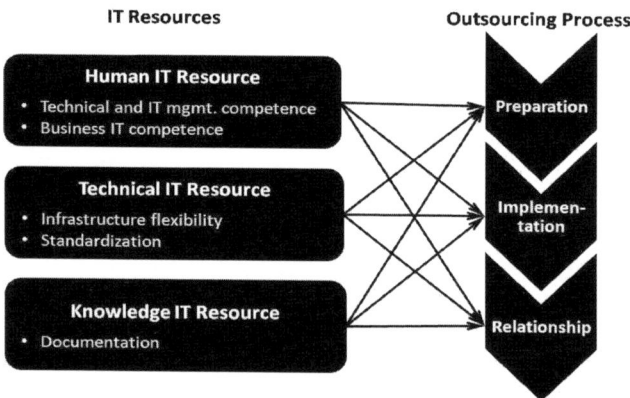

Figure 2: Research Model of Paper 3

The results are based on a series of case studies performed with senior managers from both outsourcing clients and vendors from the financial industry. As mentioned in chapter 4.1, a two-step approach was chosen for pursuing the case studies. In a first step, a case study with a large IT outsourcing provider was conducted, aiming to understand the different associations between the preparedness of the client's IT resources and the successful preparation, implementation and maintenance of IT outsourcing relationships. We chose to carry out this first set of interviews with managers from the provider side because asking provider managers with extensive experience in the outsourcing domain would allow us to collect aggregated insights from multiple outsourcing projects. Moreover, the particular firm at which the interviewed managers are employed is a large and established outsourcing provider for application management with a wide portfolio of clients of different sizes and from different branches (financial services, automotive, etc). In the second stage, we performed two case studies with client firms from the financial industry. The aim of the second stage was to validate the findings from the first stage through two representative client case studies. From the two cases, the first case was a successful outsourcing project, while the second case represented a failed outsourcing project, which had to be aborted prematurely.

The findings of this paper are manifold. They describe the mechanisms through which each type of client's IT resources impacts the outsourcing process and its outcomes. For example, the paper shows that not only the obvious types of documentation – such as source code and other forms of technical documentation – are critical for the success of IT outsourcing, but also documentation of operations (statistics about usage, peak times, errors and performance of the systems subject to outsourcing) and technology management (documentation of service processes and performed changes). Such statistics provide the necessary information base for detailed contract specification (service levels and key performance indicators, detailed pricing of the provided services etc.) and also provide valuable information to the vendor on how to operate and maintain those systems, which eventually translates into higher service quality.

Overall, this paper empirically demonstrates that explaining outsourcing success or failure may not only root in factors like incomplete or faulty outsourcing contracts, in the selection of inadequate providers or bad relationship management (as discussed in prior literature), but also depends to a large extent on the readiness of the client's internal IT resources to support outsourcing.

The findings of paper 3 are summarized in the tables below. Table 1 illustrates the ways in which the human IT resource affects outsourcing. Table 2 summarizes the impact of the technical IT resource, while table 3 discloses the impact of explicit knowledge in form of documentation on the outsourcing process.

	Dimension	Competencies	Impact on outsourcing		
			Preparation phase	Transition phase	Ongoing relationship
Human IT Resource	Technical and managerial competence	Technical		Identify hyphenation points for extracting the systems that are to be outsourced from their current technological environment	
				Perform required changes to adjacent systems which are kept in-house	
		Technology management	Formulate SLAs and KPIs; Assess criticality of systems for the overall business; Elaborate contingency plans		Monitor the output provided by the outsourcing partner
	Business Competence	Project management	Plan and manage costs, people, time, and quality criteria of outsourcing projects.		
		Leadership and interpersonal	Motivate personnel to accept and support outsourcing; disclose personal perspectives for affected employees		
		Business function	Align with business domain		
					Formulate and prioritize changes

Table 1: How the Human IT Resource affects outsourcing success

	Dimension	Aspect	Impact on outsourcing		
			Preparation phase	Transition phase	Ongoing relationship
Technical IT Resource	Flexibility	Integration	Facilitates the interconnection of the partner's systems with the own systems; enables seamless information transfer and processing between the partners		
		Modularity	Eases the identification of hyphenation points and the extraction of the systems that are subject to outsourcing from their current environment		
	Standardi-zation		Acts as an enabler for flexibility; allows for easier interconnection between partners	Reduces the need for extensive knowledge transfer between client and provider	
			Allows for a wider array of choices among specialized providers		

Table 2: How the Technical IT Resource affects outsourcing success

	Impact on outsourcing		
	Preparation phase	**Transition phase**	**Ongoing relationship**
Knowledge IT Resource: Documentation	Helps to identify necessary changes to adjacent systems and business processes; Provides information basis for contract specification and formulation of SLAs and KPIs	Helps to improve knowledge transfer between client and provider by providing a source of explicit knowledge. Alleviates to some degree the disadvantages stemming from missing standardization and modularity.	Improves provider flexibility and lowers the costs of change implementations.

Table 3: How the Knowledge IT Resource affects outsourcing success

5.4 Paper 4[4]: Quantitative Results: Empirical Evidence for the Impact of Client's Explicit Business Process Knowledge on Outsourcing Outcomes

Paper 4 investigates the role played by the client's existing *process documentation*, as a source of explicit knowledge for the provider about the client's business domain, in shaping the relationship between client and provider. *How does the availability of explicit, up-to-date process documentation influence the operational alignment between client and IT provider? How does this affect the flexibility of the provider in terms of reacting to the client's requests?* Based on a sample of 104 application management outsourcing relationships from the German banking industry, the paper draws upon the KBV (see chapter 3.2) to explore the interplay between different dimensions of alignment and IT provider's flexibility, and how the availability of qualitative, up-to-date process documentation affects these links.

The paper's main findings are:

1. The availability of reliable, up-to-date process documentation increases the client's outsourcing readiness by fostering knowledge transferability.

---

[4] Martin, S.F., Wagner, H.-T., Beimborn, D.: "Process Documentation, Operational Alignment, and Flexibility in IT Outsourcing Relationships: A Knowledge-Based Perspective". In: International Conference on Information Systems (ICIS), Paris, France, 2008.

2. The outsourcing provider implements change requests more timely and accurately when it has more knowledge about its customer's business domain.

3. Client's trust, acceptance, and respect towards the provider are strongly influenced by the level of business domain knowledge exhibited by the provider and by the flexibility with which it reacts to client's requests.

4. However, the strength of these causal relationships is strongly contingent upon the availability of reliable business process documentation. When only low levels of reliable documentation are available, the provider has the chance to create a good impression and gain the client's trust and acceptance by proving to be knowledgeable about the client's business domain. However, if up-to-date documentation is available, client's trust, acceptance, and respect are now based more on "hard facts" – like the timeliness and accuracy of provider's reactions –, while merely "speaking the client's language" becomes insufficient for building strong cognitive ties.

5.5 Paper 5[5]: Quantitative Results: Empirical Evidence for the Impact of Client-Internal IT-Business Alignment on Outsourcing Success

Paper 5, also taking a knowledge-based perspective, provides quantitative empirical confirmation for the positive impact of alignment on outsourcing success, which has been hypothesized in the earlier conceptual papers.

Especially in their incipient phase, outsourcing relationships require extensive knowledge exchange between client and provider, because the provider needs to acquire a thorough understanding of its client's specifics in terms of business processes and IT infrastructure (Dibbern et al. 2008). While the provider needs

---

[5] Martin, S.F.: "The Impact of Alignment on Outsourcing Outcomes: Empirical Evidence from the German Banking Industry". Submitted for publication to Information & Management.

the ability to integrate the knowledge received from the client (Dibbern et al. 2008; Lee 2001), it is the client's responsibility to gather relevant information internally to make it available to the IT provider. For that matter, the client is confronted with the need to internally coordinate different stakeholders from business and IT domains in order to aggregate complex and idiosyncratic knowledge, to eliminate ambiguity and to make the relevant knowledge transferable. Drawing on a sample of 160 application management outsourcing relationships from the German banking industry, the paper discusses how IT-business alignment, at an operational level, enables the client to cope with these needs, thereby enhancing its organizational outsourcing readiness. The main findings of this paper are:

1. In young outsourcing relationships, the quality of the *inter*-organizational communication between client and vendor is dependent on the quality of the *inner*-organizational communication between client's IT and business domains. This is because higher inner-organizational communication quality within the client's own organization enables a more effective and reliable transfer of client-related knowledge to the vendor. In turn, higher inter-organizational communication quality enhances the vendor's overall ability to provide prompt and reliable services.

2. In already established outsourcing relationships, thorough internal alignment allows the client to formulate change requests more precisely and accurately, which in turn fosters the provider's ability to implement changes more timely and reliably.

3. Within the client's organization, cognitive relationships (trust, mutual understanding, and respect) are the main drivers for an effective and reliable information exchange between employees from business and IT domains. The effect of cognitive ties between the two domains is significantly stronger than the positive effect of a strong common knowledge base.

6 Contribution to Theory and Practical Implications

6.1 Contribution to Theory

Papers 1 and 2 contribute to the outsourcing research literature by developing two basic models of the impact of organizational readiness and alignment on the outcomes of the inter-organizational cooperation between client and service provider. Paper 1 provides a process view while paper 2 provides a cross-sectional view on the impact of organizational readiness and alignment on outsourcing success. These papers also contribute to literature by bringing together insights from two different streams of research: on outsourcing and on alignment. Although rich literature streams exist on both IT business alignment and inter-organizational cooperation (like, e.g., outsourcing), a combined view of IS research on IT business alignment and inter-firm cooperation has been missing so far. It is for the first time that the impact of alignment, which typically refers to the firm-internal coordination of business and IT domains, is considered and evaluated in an inter-organizational context. Therefore, besides the concrete development of two theoretical models, the contribution of the conceptual papers 1 and 2 lies in bringing together those two streams of research, hereby enlarging the existing knowledge on inter-organizational cooperation by adding the new view of the impact of the client's inner-organizational context, including the role of IT business alignment, on the outcomes of outsourcing. Consequently, papers 3, 4, and 5 further develop this view by adding empirical results to this conceptual basis.

Based on the implicit RBV assumption that differences in the resources and capabilities possessed by firms lead to different levels of firm readiness for outsourcing (see chapter 3.1), **paper 3** represents one of the first empirical attempts so far to dedicatedly consider client's IT capabilities and resources as enablers or inhibitors for outsourcing success. The paper contributes to the existing literature and extends existing knowledge by depicting and structuring the ways by which client's IT resources affect the outsourcing process and ultimately outsourcing success. Its primary contribution resides in pointing out that the client's existing IT resources may play an important, if not decisive, role in each phase of the outsourcing process and that a firm's outsourcing readiness is an issue worthy of more academic and practitioner attention. The results of this paper illustrate and classify the different roles played by each of the client's IT resources along the three phases of the outsourcing process.

Paper 4 draws on the KBV (see chapter 3.2) to show how business process documentation, as a form of explicit knowledge generated within the client firm, affects the relationship between client and provider and the flexibility with which the provider may react to the client's change requests during an outsourcing relationship. The paper shows that good process documentation enhances the client organization's outsourcing readiness by fostering knowledge transferability. However, the paper also shows that explicit knowledge is only a partial substitute for tacit knowledge. Thus, while the availability of explicit knowledge in form of process documentation is important, *tacit* knowledge, which is rooted in experience, continues to play a significant role in affecting the IT provider's flexibility, even in cases where a comprehensive and up-to-date documentation is available.

Finally, **paper 5**, also drawing on KBV, provides empirical support for the hypothesis that internal alignment has a positive impact on the outsourcing relationship and implicitly on the outcomes of outsourcing. The main contribution of this paper to existing literature is the empirical insight that effective knowledge transfer depends not just on "how easily that knowledge can be transported, interpreted, and absorbed" (Simonin 1999, p.597), but also on the client's ability to coordinate different stakeholders within its own organization in order to aggregate relevant and reliable knowledge and to make it available to the provider. An additional contribution of this paper is brought by considering time, expressed as the age of the outsourcing relationship, as a contingency variable. The paper proves empirically that the impact of alignment on the relationship quality between client and provider grows weaker as the relationship becomes more mature, because the provider has had the necessary time to gain deep insights about its client, which makes the provider less dependent on the amount and quality of the information it receives from the client.

6.2 Practical Implications

The empirical analysis reveals that especially outsourcing providers are well aware of the lack of outsourcing readiness often exhibited by their clients, whereas clients often tend to overlook issues grounded within their own organization, tending to blame the provider for any failures that occur during an outsourcing venture. Therefore, a general contribution of this dissertation, especially directed towards outsourcing clients, is the empirical insight that client's outsourcing readiness, as shown on the three selected factors IT capability, IT business alignment, and explicit business process knowledge, is of crucial importance for the success of outsourcing ventures.

Considering the three empirical papers individually, paper 3 provides guidance for the assessment of the client's IT-related outsourcing readiness, facilitating the identification of potential hidden cost drivers, by specifically showing which characteristics of the IT capability come into play within which phase of the outsourcing deal. This provides managers with a more solid basis for calculating the outsourcing business case.

The main practical implication of paper 4 is that managers should foster knowledge exchange between the client and the IT service provider because it promotes the development of business understanding and orientation which helps the IT service provider to deliver flexible services. This could be done, for example, through mentoring and on-the-job trainings of the service provider's employees by dedicated client personnel and through intensive communication by means of formal meetings and joint preparation of documentation.

The main practical implication of paper 5 is that managers should not underestimate the importance of being internally aligned for achieving benefits from an outsourcing venture. Client organizations need to carefully choose the person who will be in charge with the relationship to the service provider, for this person will not only need to manage the provider, but will also need to be able to internally coordinate stakeholders from different departments and domains and to reach aligned decisions which can be communicated clearly and reliably to the provider.

7 Limitations and Further Research

There are several limitations to this thesis, which call for a careful interpretation of the results.

Generalizability and Validity of Results

First, there are limitations concerning the generalizability of the research results. Especially the qualitative research results need to be interpreted carefully, since case study research is marked by hardly replicable events and generalizability of results is inconsistent with the requirements of statistical sampling procedures. However, in case study research, limited generalizability may be reached through analytical methods. The recommendations of case study methodologists (Dubé and Paré 2003; Shanks and Parr 2003; Yin 2003), who call for the selection of "typical" cases – i.e., cases which are representative for a large number of other cases –, have been followed strictly to ensure the external validity of the research results.

Although limited external validity is less of a problem in the quantitative part of this dissertation, in which statistical remedies were employed in order to cope with this issue, generalizability of results might still suffer here from the narrow focus on only one industry. The strict and mandatory regulations pertaining to the way banks are supposed to govern their IT function and document their processes lead to a certain basic level of preparedness which is common to all banks and which may not exist in other industries. Moreover, the three pillar structure of the German banking industry, where more than 80% of all German banks are public savings banks or credit cooperatives which are organized in quite tight national associations, reflects an industry structure which is quite unique in the world. Therefore, results are not generalizable beyond the German financial industry without further ado. Hence, focusing on a particular industry as a way to achieve unbiased results, as recommended by methodologists (see chapter 2), comes at the expense of limited generalizability.

Moreover, the design of the surveys, focusing on a single person in each organization which was surveyed at a single point in time, includes the threat of Common Method Bias. This bias, although rigorously coped with through the use of ex-ante and ex-post remedies (as described in the single papers), might also affect the validity of the results.

Getting the Complete Picture

Another limitation pertains to the breadth of the organizational readiness concept covered by this dissertation, which has surely not been captured in all its integrity. However, it was not the aim of this dissertation to cover all aspects that could possibly influence an organization's readiness for outsourcing for such an endeavor would go far beyond the scope of a single dissertation. Instead, this dissertation pinpoints the influence of three selected aspects – the client's IT capability, its inner-organizational alignment, and the quality of its explicit business process knowledge – that enable the client organization to achieve its outsourcing goals more reliably, hereby making the point that a firm's inner-organizational settings may play a decisive role for achieving outsourcing success and that a firm's outsourcing readiness is an issue worthy of more academic and practitioner attention.

Beside the three factors covered by this dissertation, many other factors related to the client's internal organization, like the organizational culture which determines the values and goals shared by the firm's employees, the maturity of management processes, the employed IT architectures and the structure of the IT organization, to name a few, are worthwhile aspects that should be considered by future research in order to reach a clearer picture of what constitutes and drives organizational readiness for outsourcing. Therefore, this dissertation regards itself as only a first step into an area of outsourcing research that will help academics and practitioners alike to complement and improve the current understanding of how to successfully master outsourcing ventures.

Turning the View Around

With regard to the link between client-internal alignment and outsourcing, this dissertation has covered only "one side of the coin" by looking at how alignment affects the outcomes of outsourcing. Turning the view around, future research should also focus on the impact that outsourcing may have on alignment.

Clients often conduct outsourcing projects and keep outsourcing relationships with many different providers. To what extent are the different outsourcing projects performed by an organization consistent? If one outsourcing project forces the client to perform certain changes to its inner-organizational structure, processes and systems, and another project is forcing it to perform other changes, are the outcomes of those changes compatible or is the organization running the risk of being pulled into different, incompatible directions? Even if each single project may be in fit with the organization's settings, collectively they might not be. Thus, it may be a worthwhile question to ask how performing different outsourcing projects which impact the firm on different levels is going to reset the strategic as well as the operational alignment within the client organization.

Entering New Research Grounds

The increasing diffusion of service-oriented architectures among today's organizations and the growing modularity of IT systems, which facilitate the flexible alteration and decomposition of the business processes they support (Krafzig et al. 2004), disclose the potential for conducting research targeted at *firms' readiness for embracing new forms of BPO*, which are not common industry practice so far. An exemplary, specific new form of BPO, which offers promising research potential, is the cooperation between banks (taking on the role of specialized service providers) and client organizations operating outside the financial industry. For such organizations, financial processes usually represent secondary processes (Porter 1985), while for banks, they represent primary processes and often even a core competence. This specific form of BPO refers to particular activities from a client organization's financial processes (e.g., cash management, electronic bill presentment and payment) being fulfilled by a bank or other specialized financial provider in an automated manner by means of inter-organizational systems. This new kind of cooperation between banks and non-financial organizations, termed "Value Chain Crossing" (VCC) in prior articles (Beimborn, Martin, Franke 2008; Beimborn, Martin, Homann 2006; König, Beimborn, Martin, Blumenberg, Homann 2007), is only possible if the client's IT architectures and systems allow for an effortless, modular decomposition of its financial business processes. Thus, for VCC to become feasible, client firms need to become technically – and also culturally – "ready".

As the above references suggest, first incursions into this promising research area have already been performed (see Appendix for a list of publications). In 2005, researchers from Cluster 1 of the E-Finance Lab have conducted a series of case studies with 11 small and mid-sized enterprises (SMEs) from outside the financial industry, aiming to assess the e-Business potential of VCC and to identify factors that affected the readiness and willingness of SMEs to adopt VCC. One of the main findings of this case study series was that some of the participating firms missed the necessary organizational readiness for outsourcing parts of their financial processes to specialized service providers, while others already featured to some degree the technical ability for such cooperation but missed the necessary *confidence* that VCC could prove feasible and that banks would have the necessary industry competence to provide such services. Thus, identifying viable scenarios for VCC, which consider the actual state of readiness of the potential partners as well as potential benefits and risks for the cooperating organizations, could prove to be a worthwhile academic endeavor which would enable IS scholars to pursue valuable research *ahead* of practice, instead of lagging behind it.

8 References

Alavi, M., and Leidner, D.E. "Review: Knowledge Management and Knowledge Management Systems: Conceptual Foundations and Research Issues," *MIS Quarterly* (25:1) 2001, pp 107-136.

BaFin "Auslagerung von Bereichen auf ein anderes Unternehmen gemäß§ 25a Abs. 2 KWG. Rundschreiben 11/2001," B.f. Finanzdienstleistungsaufsicht (ed.), Bonn, 2001.

Barney, J.B. "Firm resources and sustained competitive advantage," *Journal of Management* (17) 1991, pp 99-120.

Barney, J.B. "Resource-based theories of competitive advantage: A ten-year retrospective on the resource-based view," *Journal of Management* (27:6) 2001, pp 643-650.

Barthélemy, J. "The Hidden Costs of IT Outsourcing," *MIT Sloan Management Review* (42:3) 2001.

Beimborn, D., Martin, S.F., and Franke, J. "Value Chain Crossing: Insights and Opportunities for Future Research," *International Journal of Electronic Business*) 2008.

Beimborn, D., Martin, S.F., and Homann, U. "Value Chain Crossing Between SMEs and the Banking Industry," The Fifth International Conference on Electronic Business (ICEB 2005), Hong Kong, 2006.

Bharadwaj, A.S. "A Resource-based Perspective on Information Technology Capability and Firm Performance: An Empirical Investigation," *MIS Quarterly* (24:1) 2000, pp 169-195.

BIS "The Joint Forum - Outsourcing in Financial Services," Bank for International Settlements, Basel, 2005.

Blumenberg, S. "A Relational View on IT Outsourcing: Identifying Dimensions and Determinants of Relationship Quality." Dissertation Thesis, Department of Business Informatics, Goethe-Universität, Frankfurt am Main, Germany, 2008.

Chiasson, M.W., and Davidson, E. "Taking Industry Seriously in Information Systems Research," *MIS Quarterly* (29:4) 2005, pp 591-605.

Chin, W.W. "The Partial Least Square Approach to Structural Equation Modeling," in: *Modern Methods for Business Research*, G.A. Marcoulides (ed.), Lawrence Erlbaum Associates, Mahwah, NJ, USA, 1998.

Dibbern, J., Goles, T., Hirschheim, R., and Jayatilaka, B. "Information systems outsourcing: A survey and analysis of the literature," *The DATA BASE for Advances in Information Systems* (35:4) 2004, pp 6-102.

Dibbern, J., Winkler, J., and Heinzl, A. "Explaining Variations in Client Extra Costs between Software Projects Offshored to India," *MIS Quarterly* (32:2) 2008, pp 333-366.

Dubé, L., and Paré, G. "Rigor in information systems positivist case research: current practices, trends, and recommendations," *MIS Quarterly* (27:4) 2003, pp 597-635.

Eisenhardt, K.M. "Building theories from case study research," *Academy of Management Review* (14:4) 1989, pp 532-550.

Fröschl, F. "Vom IuK-Outsourcing zum Business Process Outsourcing," *Wirtschaftsinformatik* (41:5) 1999, pp 458-460.

Gellings, C. "Outsourcing Relationships: Designing Contracts for Successful Outsourcing." Dissertation Thesis, Department of Business Informatics, Goethe-Universität, Frankfurt am Main, Germany, 2007.

Gewald, H., and Franke, J. "The risks of business process outsourcing: a two-fold assessment in the German banking industry," *International Journal of Electronic Finance* (1:4) 2007, pp 420-441.

Goles, T., and Chin, W.W. "Information Systems Outsourcing Relationship Factors: Detailed Conceptualization and Initial Evidence," *The DATA BASE for Advances in Information Systems* (36:4) 2005, pp 47-67.

Goo, J., Kishore, R., Rao, H.R., and Nam, K. "The Role of Service Level Agreements in Relational Management of Information Technology Outsourcing: An Empirical Study," *MIS Quarterly* (33:1) 2009, pp 119-145.

Gopal, A., Bostrom, R.P., and Chin, W.W. "Applying Adaptive Structuration Theory to Investigate the Process of Group Support Systems Use," *Journal of Management Information Systems* (9:3) 1993, pp 45-69.

Grant, R.M. "Toward a knowledge-based theory of the firm," *Strategic Management Journal* (17:10) 1996, pp 109-122.

Hirschheim, R.A. "Interview wit Rudy Hirschheim on "Perception on information systems outsourcing"," *Wirtschaftsinformatik* (45:2) 2003, pp 111-114.

Kogut, B., and Zander, U. "Knowledge of the Firm, Combinative Capabilities, and the Replication of Technology," *Organization Science* (3:3) 1992, pp 383-397.

König, W., Beimborn, D., Martin , S., Blumenberg, S., and Homann, U. "Mittelständler und Banken: Einflussfaktoren der Bereitschaft zur Kooperation auf der Basis eingebetteter Informationssysteme," in: *Architekturen und Prozesse. Strukturen und Dynamik in Forschung und Unternehmen,* P. Loos and H. Krcmar (eds.), Springer, Berlin, 2007.

Krafzig, D., Banke, K., and Slama, D. *Enterprise SOA: Service-Oriented Architecture Best Practices* Prentice Hall International, 2004.

Kraus, M. "Der Markt für IT-Services in Deutschland, 2007-2012," IDC Central Europe GmbH.

Lacity, M.C., Willcocks, L.P., and Feeny, D.F. "The Value of Selective IT Sourcing," *Sloan Management Review* (37:1) 1996, pp 13-25.

Lancellotti, R., Schein, O., Spang, S., and Stadler, V. "ICT and Operations outsourcing in banking - Insights from an interview-based pan-European survey," *Wirtschaftsinformatik* (45:2) 2003, pp 131-141.

Lee, J.N. "The impact of knowledge sharing, organizational capability and partnership quality on IS outsourcing success," *Information & Management* (38:5) 2001, pp 323-335.

McFarlan, F., and Nolan, R. "How to manage an IS outsourcing alliance," *Sloan Management Review* (36:2) 1995, pp 9-23.

Michell, V., and Fitzgerald, G. "The IT outsourcing market-place: vendors and their selection," *Journal of Information Technology* (12) 1997, pp 223-237.

Nonaka, I. "A Dynamic Theory of Organizational Knowledge Creation," *Organization Science* (5:1) 1994, pp 14-37.

Penrose, E.T. *The theory of the growth of the firm* Wiley, New York, 1959.

Porter, M.E. *Competitive Advantage. Creating and Sustaining Superior Performance.* Free Press, New York, 1985.

Qureshi, I., and Compeau, D. "Assessing Between-Group Differences in Information Systems Research: A Comparison of Covariance- and Component-Based SEM," *MIS Quarterly* (33:1) 2009, pp 197-214.

Ranganathan, C., and Balaji, S. "Critical Capabilities for Offshore Outsourcing of Information Systems," *MIS Quarterly Executive* (6:3), September 2007, pp 147-164.

Ross, J.W., and Westerman, G. "Preparing for utility computing: The role of IT architecture and relationship management," *IBM Systems Journal* (43:1) 2004, pp 5-19.

Rouse, A.C., and Corbitt, B. "IT-supported business process outsourcing (BPO): The good, the bad, and the ugly," 8th Pacific-Asia Conference on Information Systems (PACIS), Shanghai, China, 2004.

Shanks, G., and Parr, A. "Positivist, Single Case Study Research in Information Systems: a Critical Analysis," in: *11th European Conference on Information Systems (ECIS 2003)*, Naples, Italy, 2003.

Simonin, B.L. "Ambiguity and the Process of Knowledge Transfer in Strategic Alliances," *Strategic Management Journal* (20:7), July 1999, pp 595-623.

Spanos, Y.E., and Lioukas, S. "An examination into the causal logic of rent generation: contrasting Porter's competitive strategy framework and the resource-based perspective," *Strategic Management Journal* (22:10) 2001, pp 907-934.

Tiwana, A. "Knowledge Partitioning in Outsourced Software Development: A Field Study," International Conference on Information Systems (ICIS), Seattle, Washington, 2003.

Wernerfelt, B. "A resource-based view of the firm," *Strategic Management Journal* (5:2) 1984, pp 171-180.

Yin, R.K. *Case study research. Design and methods*, (3rd ed.) Sage Publications, Beverly Hills, CA, 2003.

Getting Ready for Success:
May Alignment Be of Help?[1]

Sebastian F. Martin
E-Finance Lab
Institute for Information Systems
Goethe University, Frankfurt,
Germany
smartin@wiwi.uni-frankfurt.de

Daniel Beimborn
E-Finance Lab
Institute for Information Systems
Goethe University, Frankfurt,
Germany
beimborn@wiwi.uni-frankfurt.de

Mihir A. Parikh
College of Business Administration
University of Central Florida, USA
mihir.parikh@bus.ucf.edu

Tim Weitzel
Chair of Information Systems
Bamberg University, Germany
tweitzel@wiwi.uni-frankfurt.de

Abstract

What is the role of organizational readiness and IT business alignment in the adoption process of an IT-supported inter-organizational linkage (IOL)? In this paper, we claim that achieving a proper level of organizational readiness is crucial for the successful adoption of IOL. We thus focus on intra-organizational factors that potentially impact the effectiveness of preparatory activities towards getting ready for the adoption and implementation of an IOL. By drawing upon results from alignment and adoption of innovations literatures, we develop and theoretically underpin a model that illustrates the moderating impact of IT business alignment on both, the initiation and implementation stages of the IOL adoption process.

---

[1] This paper has been published in the Proceedings of the 13th Americas Conference on Information Systems (AMCIS 2007), Keystone (CO), USA, 2007

1 Introduction

Although IT-supported cooperation among firms is a phenomenon which has emerged many years ago and currently is a wide-spread practice in many industries, we can still find many examples of cooperative relationships (like sourcing relationships, for example) which fail to deliver the expected benefits (Aubert and Patry 1998; Goles and Chin 2005). Many reasons for this may occur, some of them being grounded within the own organization. This shows that careful preparations such as the adaptation of firm-internal business processes – including the underlying IT – are necessary in order for firms to be able to reap the benefits from inter-organizational cooperation. There is indication from literature that a proper level of organizational readiness is important for the achievement of positive outcomes from IT-based cooperation (Iacovou et al. 1995). Nevertheless, the question what (intra-)organizational factors are of particular importance when adopting a new inter-organizational linkage (IOL), has received surprisingly little attention from academics. The correct assessment of the own organizational readiness and the effective execution of preparative activities towards the achievement of a sufficient level of organizational readiness are difficult tasks to be carried out because they require the tight and well-coordinated collaboration of individuals from different departments as well as different organizations.

In this paper, we focus on the intra-organizational collaboration of IT and business departments (so-called IT business alignment – ITBA) within an IOL-adopting organization. We refer to an IOL as inter-organizational cooperation by means of inter-organizational systems (IOS) (Teo et al. 2003).

Alignment between IT and business domain in organizations has been discussed to substantially contribute to the generation of competitive advantage by means of knowledge sharing and integration (Kearns and Lederer 2003; Reich and Benbasat 2000). In order to be successful, the establishment of an IOL requires the involvement of both organizational layers: the business unit as well as the IT unit, which have to collaborate in a tight and aligned way during the IOL evaluation and implementation process.

There are different knowledge pools within the firm (i.e. business side and IT domain) (Reich and Benbasat 2000) which have to be incorporated into the process of evaluating the potential of an IOL and further to enable its successful adoption. Through its underlying routines, alignment represents a continuous process of knowledge sharing and creation, where individual knowledge is transformed into organizational know-how and behavior. We claim that in situations where the organization adopts an innovation which affects both, the business as well as the IT domain, good IT business alignment may contribute to IOL adoption success. Our main propositions are (1) that high organizational readiness is crucial for the successful implementation of an IOL and (2) that IT business alignment positively affects a firm's capability to identify opportunities for IOL and to reap the benefits from IOL by enabling it to effectively adapt its organizational structure and IT to meet the demands of the new cooperation. The more intense the interplay between business and IT domain within an organization (i.e. the higher the level of ITBA in terms of formal and informal routines), the more capable will an organization be to correctly evaluate the fit between a prospective IOL and the firm's goals, structure, and financial and technological possibilities (i.e. its organizational readiness to adopt IOL) and, subsequently, the more effective it will implement the necessary changes on structural and IT level in order to become ready for the specific IOL.

Therefore, the research questions guiding the development of this paper are:

What is the impact of organizational readiness on the intention to adopt and the eventual success of an IOL?

How does intra-organizational IT business alignment affect a firm's IOL adoption process?

For this purpose, we develop and theoretically underpin a model that captures the relationships between organizational readiness, IOL adoption intention, IOL success, and IT business alignment, mapping them on the different stages of a generic innovation adoption process. Answers to these questions will contribute to the existing body of knowledge by allowing us to gain deeper insights into organizational factors which act as drivers for the successful adoption and implementation of IOL.

2 Literature Review

2.1 Adoption of Innovations

The adoption of IT-based IOL has often been discussed from an adoption and diffusion of innovations perspective (e.g., Khalifa and Davison 2006; Saunders and Clark 1992; e.g., Teo et al. 2003). Under the "dominant paradigm" (Fichman 2004), authors are mainly interested in identifying factors that either inhibit or facilitate the adoption of innovations like IT-based IOL. For example, Teo et al. (2003) found isomorphic pressures (mimetic, coercive, and normative) to positively influence IOL adoption intention. Khalifa and Davison (2006) distinguished between internal and external pressures and further found perceived feasibility and perceived desirability of IOL to significantly influence managerial IOL adoption intention. Organizational readiness (in terms of financial and human resources, processes, IT sophistication, etc.) has also been found to significantly influence the adoption of IT-based IOL (Chwelos et al. 2001; Iacovou et al. 1995). Furthermore, readiness of the trading partner has been found to be an enabler for the adoption of IOS (Chang and Chen 2005; Chwelos et al. 2001).

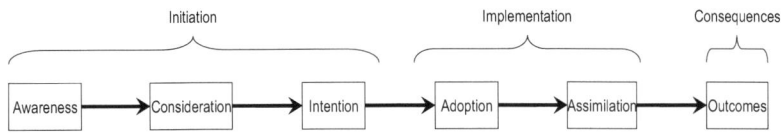

Figure 1: Innovation process (based on Frambach and Schillewaert 2002; Gallivan 2001)

The organizational innovation process has been discussed to be a sequence of different stages and substages (as depicted by Figure 1). "In the initiation stage, the organization becomes aware of the innovation, forms an attitude towards it, and evaluates the new product; it encompasses awareness, consideration, and intention substages. In the implementation stage, the organization decides to purchase and make use of the innovation. [...] the acceptance or assimilation within the organization now becomes important" (Frambach and Schillewaert 2002, p. 164). After the implementation stage, organizational consequences may be observed (Gallivan 2001). The pre-adoption stages (awareness, consideration and intention) as well as the outcomes of adoption have repeatedly been claimed to be under-researched (Fichman 2004; Frambach and Schillewaert 2002; Jeyaraj et al. 2006). We contribute to closing this gap by analyzing how IT business alignment impacts the initiation stage as well as the consequences of IOL adoption.

2.2 IT Business Alignment

Alignment was found to be an important factor for generating business value from the deployment of information systems (Chan et al. 1997; Papp 1999; Teo and King 1996). Based on the Strategic Alignment Model (Henderson and Venkatraman 1993), research has focused primarily on antecedents or enablers and inhibitors of alignment (Luftman et al. 1999). According to Reich and Benbasat (1996), ITBA is "the degree to which the information technology mission, objectives, and plans support and are supported by the business mission, objectives and plans". Their model of alignment consists of an intellectual and a social dimension. The intellectual dimension is a refinement of content linkage as defined by Lederer and Mendelow (1989), differentiating between internal consistency (IT mission is internally consistent with business mission) and external validity (plans are comprehensive and valid with respect to external business and IT environment). In contrast, the social dimension describes "the level of mutual understanding of and commitment to the business and IT mission, objectives and plans". The social dimension of alignment is driven by cross-domain knowledge between business and IT executives, IT implementation success, effective communication between business and IT executives, and connections between business and IT planning processes (Reich and Benbasat 2000). Tiwana et al. (2003) add a cognitive dimension which covers psychological relationship issues such as trust, mutual understanding, and commitment.

The different alignment facets distinguish between alignment as an outcome and alignment as a process which affects the outcome dimensions (Sabherwal and Chan 2001). The most prominent argument for the latter stems from Kearns and Lederer (2003, p. 5) who state that alignment is a "process in which managers participate in the exchange of knowledge". Thus, alignment describes effective communication and knowledge exchange patterns (routines) which affect the outcome dimensions of shared knowledge and mutual understanding and lead to the fit of business and IT strategies and plans (Bergeron et al. 2004). Several authors link alignment to the resource-based view and describe it as a dynamic capability to develop and implement congruent IT and business plans (e.g., Sambamurthy and Zmud 1999; e.g., Wagner and Weitzel 2005). The alignment process itself is based on the concept of routines which describe the formal and informal purposeful interaction of entities within an organization (Amit and Schoemaker 1993). "Smoothly functioning routines between IT and business units are seen as valuable leading to a more effective development and use of IT" (Wagner and Weitzel 2005, p. 4).

Prior research has identified two primary consequences of alignment: increased IS effectiveness (Chan et al. 1997) and increased firm performance (Sabherwal and Chan 2001). In contrast, misalignment of business and IT has been found to lead to undesirable organizational effects like poor utilization of scarce organizational resources, sub-optimal performance of business units and the organization, a cyclical relationship between higher IS spending and expectations for success, costly IS investments with low yield returns, missed identification of high potential IS applications, and lack of capitalization of first-rate technology-related ideas (Chan 2002; Lederer and Mendelow 1987).

3   Model Development

Figure 2 depicts our research model. We will discuss the constructs and the way they interrelate in the following sections.

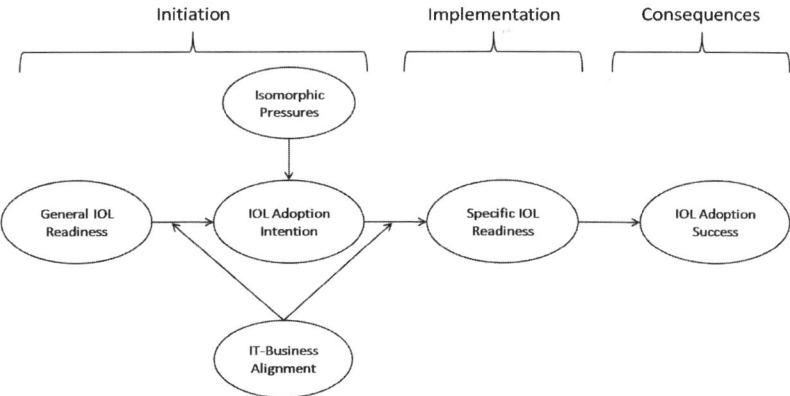

Figure 2: Research Model

3.1 IOL Adoption Intention

IOL adoption intention refers to the organizational decision to enter an IT-based, inter-organizational cooperation. Although it is ultimately individuals who will trigger it, organizational intention is formed as a consensus of the key decision-makers towards performing the behavior in question, i.e., IOL adoption. Adoption intention has been the dependent variable in some recent studies (Khalifa and Davison 2006; Plouffe et al. 2001; Teo et al. 2003) and has usually been measured by capturing managerial perceptions.

3.2 Isomorphic Pressures

Isomorphic pressures refer to external and/or internal coercive, mimetic and normative pressures experienced by the organization. Institutional theory (DiMaggio and Powell 1983; Meyer and Rowan 1977; Scott 2001; Teo et al. 2003) provides a powerful lens to examine how organizations sense threats and react to them. It views organizational design not as a rational process but the result of organizational reactions to external and/or internal pressures that prompt organizations in an organizational field to resemble one another over time. This isomorphic behavior is considered a key factor affecting an organization's intention to adopt an IOL.

3.3 IOL Readiness

IOL readiness reflects the structural and technical capability of a firm to adopt IOL. Similar conceptualizations have been used by many researchers. For example, Iacovou et al. (1995) use organizational readiness in their model of EDI adoption as "the level of financial and technological resources of the firm". Within their TOE framework, Kuan and Chau (2001) refer to readiness as perceived organizational resources.

Our concept of IOL readiness consists of two dimensions or layers: a business and an IT dimension:

The business dimension, termed *IOR (inter-organizational relationship) readiness*, reflects the structural preparedness of the firm to adopt an IOL. It implies the adaptation of processes to meet the needs of the IOR, the redistribution of authority and responsibilities, etc.

The IT dimension, termed *IOS (inter-organizational systems) readiness*, reflects the technological preparedness of the firm in terms of IT sophistication and know how to either adopt new, or adapt an existing IOS in order to technologically support the IOR.

In our model, we further differentiate between *general* IOL readiness, which refers to the general state of preparedness of the organization to adopt *any* IOL and *specific* IOL readiness which refers to the specific IOL relationship for which we are measuring adoption intention and adoption success. Along the innovation process, general IOL readiness refers to the state of readiness within the initiation stage, at the time when the firm becomes aware of the opportunity or necessity to enter an IOL. This general IOL readiness may be, as we will discuss later, an enabler of IOL adoption intention. In contrast, specific IOL readiness is the state of preparedness *after* the firm has taken the decision to adopt IOL and has conducted preparatory actions for the specific IOL.

3.4 IT Business Alignment

In this paper, we draw on both the intellectual dimension and social dimension of alignment (Reich and Benbasat 1996) as well as on their interrelations. Since the *intellectual dimension* reflects the match of IT and business strategies, concepts, and plans, it represents the common organizational frame or environment that forms the foundation for innovation adoption processes.

The *social dimension* of ITBA – as introduced above – is a complex construct which consists of various dimensions. Beimborn et al. (2006a; 2006b) developed an operational alignment construct consisting of the dimensions of *shared knowledge*, *communication*, and *cognitive relationship* for exploring the impact of operational alignment on effective usage of usage and, subsequently, on process performance. Since *this* research work focuses on the adoption of IOL, we further add the remaining dimensions from Reich and Benbasat (2000) which are *connections* between business and IT planning processes and *IT implementation success*. Figure 3 clarifies the construct layout.

A major advantage of the explicit consideration of different dimensions and sub-dimensions of such a pivotal construct is that it allows for measuring the singular impact of each particular dimension on the different steps of the innovation adoption process.

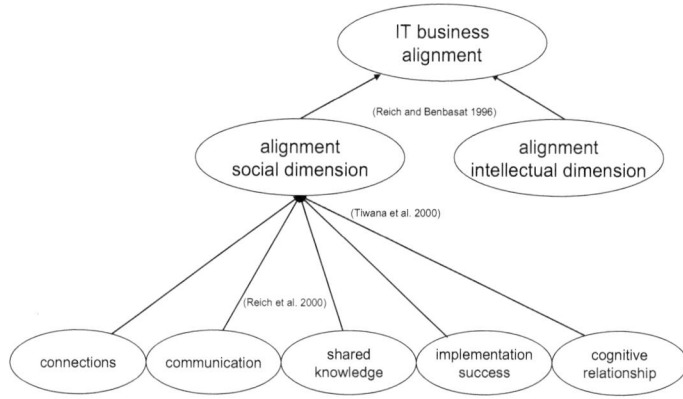

Figure 3: IT business alignment construct

Connections measures the relation between IT and business planning processes (Reich and Benbasat 2000). Lederer and Burky (1989) and Zmud (1988) found evidence that tight interconnections between IT and business units during the introduction of new technologies (e.g. by implementing technology transfer groups and joint steering committees (Reich and Benbasat 2000)) are critical fur successful implementation of IT.

The second part of the social dimension – *communication* – refers to the kind and quality of interaction patterns and communication channels between IT and business unit in the daily business. What are the formal and informal relations between the people of the different organizational units? How effectively are different communication channels being used?

The *shared knowledge* dimension represents the ability to understand the opposite (business or IT) domain (Nelson and Cooprider 1996). Business employees' knowledge positively affects the relationship (Broadbent and Weill 1993) as well as business-related knowledge of IT managers does (Sambamurthy and Zmud 1997). The latter is sometimes categorized as part of the IT's absorptive capacity in the literature (Boynton et al. 1994). Do IT employees have an understanding for the business structure and processes which are provided by them? Do they have an understanding for the specific problems of the business domain which have to be solved by joint initiatives?

Success of IT projects represents a further facet of the social dimension (Reich and Benbasat 2000) and can also be seen as an enabler for the *cognitive relationship*. Concepts like trust, mutual respect, mutual acceptance, and mutual understanding of common goals form the critical foundation of a good relationship between IT and business people (Galunic and Rodan 1998; Nelson and Cooprider 1996; Tiwana et al. 2003).

Obviously, the different dimensions of alignment are interdependent and affect each other. For example, the cognitive relationship can be seen both as a driver as well as an outcome of all remaining social dimension facets (Hansen 1999; Tiwana et al. 2003).

The *intellectual dimension* can be measured as a single item measure, as applied in recent studies (Beimborn et al. 2006b; Tallon et al. 2000b). In contrast, the social dimension with its five sub-dimensions is considered as a second-order construct with the sub-dimensions being latent variables as well. Indicators can be adopted from (Bassellier and Benbasat 2004; Bhatt 2003; Broadbent and

Weill 1993; Chung et al. 2003; Luftman 2000; Reich and Benbasat 1996; Teo and King 1996).

3.5 IOL Adoption Success

IOL adoption success measures the result of the adoption process. It represents the organization's realized benefits from adopting the IOL. Adoption success can be conceptualized as the difference between the expected benefits (before adoption) and the realized benefits (after adoption) of IOL. IOL success can be measured by collecting both perceptual measures from the managers in charge with the business process (assuming that these managers are sufficiently informed about the constructs in question (Wagner 2006)) as well as objective measures (Venkatraman and Ramanujam 1987). Perceptual measures are a widely accepted mode of operationalization of constructs in IS research, because there is evidence that these measures strongly correlate with objective measures (Powell and Dent-Micallef 1997; Tallon et al. 2000a).

4 Propositions

Organizational readiness has been previously shown to be a driver of IOL adoption intention (Chwelos et al. 2001; Iacovou et al. 1995). Conceptually, IOL adoption intention may be the result of either one of the two following triggering events, or a combination of both. First, the organization may identify opportunities for change which could help the organization to achieve its efficiency goals (Khalifa and Davison 2006). Therefore, after becoming aware of the opportunity and evaluating it, the firm may decide to adopt the IOL. Second, intention to adopt IOL may arise as response to isomorphic pressures (Teo et al. 2003). While the first situation can be seen as a reaction to opportunities, the second represents a reaction to threats: "in highly competitive markets, innovation adoption may be necessary to maintain one's market position. Non-adoption of an innovation [...] in such an environment may result in competitive disadvantage" (Frambach and Schillewaert 2002, p. 167).

Similar indications for the antecedents of intention can be found in prior literature. For example, referring to the initiation stage of the innovation process, Cooper & Zmud (1990, p. 124) state that change may evolve "from either organizational need (pull), technological innovation (push) or both". Teo et al. (2003) found isomorphic pressures (coercive, mimetic, and normative) to have a significant impact on IOL adoption intention. Also, Khalifa & Davison (2006, p. 277) note that "while isomorphic pressures are undeniably relevant to the organizational adoption decision [...], organizations also adopt IT when they anticipate significant benefits, e.g., efficiency gains, and are positive about their readiness, e.g., financial, technological, and organizational feasibility". Kuan and Chau (2001, p. 511) state: "if the perceived benefits cannot be achieved due to lack of resources, adoption is meaningless to the company regardless of how great the benefits are". Therefore, we formulate:

P1 Higher levels of IOL readiness lead to higher IOL adoption intention.

P2 Higher levels of isomorphic pressures lead to higher IOL adoption intention.

After deciding to adopt a specific IOL, the organization needs to make the necessary preparations for its implementation. Both, business and IT domain are affected by this, with the degree of change depending on their prior state of preparedness. Kantor (1994) noted that IOR alter "internal roles, relationships, and power dynamics for the organizations entering into them". Indeed, on a structural level, to be capable to meet the specific demands and reap the benefits from the new cooperation, the firm needs to redistribute responsibilities and rearrange existing, or instantiate new, routines for dealing with the new external and the changed internal arrangements (Loh and Venkatraman 1992). At a technical level, the firm needs to adapt the existing infrastructure and possibly adopt new IOS to ensure smooth data exchange with the IOL partner. Therefore, we claim that

P3 IOL adoption intention is a direct driver of IOL readiness.

Focusing dedicatedly on our research questions, we now incorporate the IT business alignment construct into our model. Basically, we propose that this intra-organizational relation between IT and business units has an important impact on the IOL adoption process (IOR and IOS), since both parties are highly involved. In the literature, there are several indications in literature that IT business alignment may have an impact on the organizational adoption of innovations. For example, Henderson and Sifonis (1988) claimed that strategic ITBA facilitates more *rational* investments in IT and reduces improvident spending. Daft (1978) argues that organizations have dual cores – administrative and technical – and that organizations vary in the relative innovativeness and degree of coupling between these cores. He claims that there are some characteristics which act as facilitators for organizational adoption of innovations – among them the "involvement in professional organizations and a high intensity of communication within organization groups" (Daft 1978, p. 207). Further, he states that "administrative innovations often affect the technical core. Hence, this type of innovation activity will be most successful when the technical core is tightly coupled to the administrative core" (Daft 1978, p. 208).

ITBA has been shown to positively influence IT flexibility, which in turn drives organizational flexibility (Wagner and Weitzel 2006). Organizational flexibility (Evans 1991) is a dynamic capability which enables firms to (proactively) screen their environment for innovation opportunities, evaluate the fit between the innovation and the company's goals, resources, and processes and, after deciding to adopt, to (reactively) rearrange their processes and resources in order to effectively reap the benefits from the innovation adoption. There is a striking resemblance between this concept and Kessler's (2004, p. 283) definition of the innovation process as "the product of both more proactive, design decisions that enable innovation and more reactive, behavioral decisions that execute innovation".

Moreover, (Beimborn et al. 2006b) have shown that IT flexibility can be enhanced by IT business alignment by means of increasing business knowledge availability to the IT domain as a result of knowledge sharing and dissemination. The basis for these effects is the structural linkage provided by frequent interaction between the IT and the business domain which facilitates knowledge sharing and mutual understanding. We thus hypothesize that by enhancing organizational flexibility

P4 ITBA positively moderates the effect of general IOL readiness on IOL adoption intention.

P5 ITBA positively moderates the effect of IOL adoption intention on specific IOL readiness.

To our knowledge, the relationship between readiness and adoption success has not been the object of explicit scholar attention so far. (As a matter of fact, there are very few articles focusing on organizational outcomes or benefits of innovation at all (Fichman 2004; Jeyaraj et al. 2006)). However, several implicit comments on this topic can be found in literature. For example, Klein and Sorra (1996) claim that the implementation effectiveness depends on the skills of employees and on the "absence of obstacles" within the organization which can be interpreted as organizational readiness. Furthermore, the compatibility of the innovation with the organization has emerged in prior literature as a critical variable for the successful adoption of an innovation (Ramamurthy 1994). Of course, a flexible organization may foster compatibility and thus increase chances for successful adoption by adapting its processes and (IT) infrastructure, i.e., creating organizational readiness for the innovation. Our last proposition thus is

P6 Higher levels of specific IOL readiness directly and positively affect IOL adoption success.

5 Conclusion and Further Research

In this paper, we developed a research model that captures the leveraging effect of ITBA on different stages of the IOL adoption process. This model and the subsequent empirical validation will enhance our understanding of the organizational factors that affect the IOL adoption process by integrating findings from the IT business alignment literature with findings from the adoption of innovations stream of research.

As a limitation of the depicted model, we should state that we are aware that there also might be a moderating effect of IT business alignment on the link between specific IOL readiness and IOL adoption success. This effect however is out of the focus of our paper, because it implies issues of intra-organizational individual-level acceptance of the innovation which we have not discussed in this paper. Moreover, the model does not incorporate other adoption-relevant factors which are important in an inter-organizational context – such as the relationship between the firms and the capabilities and attitudes of the partner firm.

Since the constructs and some of the hypotheses are already well grounded in theory, the appropriate research paradigm for the empirical validation of the proposed model is positivism. Nevertheless, within the positivist context we want to get deeper insights about what are the relevant facets of the chosen constructs in the relevant context of IOL adoption and therefore propose a sequential data collection process of both case studies and a subsequent quantitative approach which is fed by the case study results, as claimed for by Mingers (2001). For example, little is known about what exactly constitutes organizational readiness for IOL. We will carefully screen existing literature and derive dimensions and indicators for this construct. The case studies will then help us to assess the relevance of the different dimensions within expert interviews. In a later step, these dimensions will be validated within a quantitative survey.

Since the research model covers a process of adopting IOL, the case studies are required to fulfill two more criteria. First, they have to be conducted over a certain period of time since the whole process has to be accompanied by *repeatedly* measuring the different constructs and testing the propositions during the adoption process. Second, the case studies will also have to incorporate the counterpart, i.e. the firm which is the partner in the inter-organizational linkage.

The case studies are intended to give valuable insights for the design of the subsequent quantitative data collection step. By testing the proposed and refined research model, we hope to contribute to a more comprehensive understanding of IOL adoption from two antipodal perspectives: (1) how does intra-organizational IT business alignment contribute to an efficient and effective process of adopting IOL (i.e. alignment research perspective), and (2) what drives successful IOL adoption?

6 Acknowledgement

This work was developed as part of a research project of the E-Finance Lab, Frankfurt am Main, Germany. We are indebted to the participating universities and industry partners.

7 References

Amit, R., and Schoemaker, P.: Strategic assets and organizational rent. In: Strategic Management Journal (14) 1993, pp. 33-46.

Aubert, B.A., and Patry, M., Rivard, S.: Assessing the Risk of IT Outsourcing. 31st Hawaii International Conference on System Sciences (HICSS-31), IEEE Computer Society, Honolulu, USA, 1998.

Bassellier, G., and Benbasat, I.: Business competence of information technology professionals: conceptual development and influence on IT-business partnerships. In: MIS Quarterly (28:4) 2004, pp. 6733-6694.

Beimborn, D., Franke, J., Gomber, P., Wagner, H.-T., and Weitzel, T.: Die Bedeutung des Alignments von IT und Fachressourcen in Finanzprozessen: Eine empirische Untersuchung. In: Wirtschaftsinformatik (48:5) 2006a, pp. 331-339.

Beimborn, D., Franke, J., Wagner, H.-T., and Weitzel, T.: Strategy matters - The role of strategy type for IT business value. 12th Americas Conference on Information Systems (AMCIS), Acapulco, Mexico, 2006b.

Bergeron, F., Raymond, L., and Rivard, S.: Ideal patterns of strategic alignment and business performance. In: Information & Management (41:8) 2004, pp. 1003-1020.

Bhatt, G.D.: Managing information systems competence for competitive advantage: an empirical analysis. 24th International Conference on Information Systems (ICIS), Seattle (WA), 2003, pp. 134-142.

Boynton, A.C., Zmud, R.W., and Jacobs, G.C.: The influence of IT management practice on IT use in large organizations. In: MIS Quarterly (18:3) 1994, pp. 299-318.

Broadbent, M., and Weill, P.: Improving business and information strategy alignment: learning from the banking industry. In: IBM Systems Journal (32:1) 1993, pp. 223-246.

Chan, Y.E.: Why haven't we mastered alignment? The importance of the informal organization structure. In: MIS Quarterly Executive (1:2) 2002, pp. 97-112.

Chan, Y.E., Huff, A.S., Barclay, D.W., and Copeland, D.G.: Business strategic orientation, information systems strategic orientation, and strategic alignment. In: Information Systems Research (8:2) 1997, pp. 125-150.

Chang, H.L., and Chen, S.H.: Assessing the Readiness of Internet-Based IOS and Evaluating Its Impact on Adoption. In: System Sciences, 2005. HICSS'05. Proceedings of the 38th Annual Hawaii International Conference on) 2005, pp. 207b-207b.

Chung, S.H., Rainer, R.K., and Lewis, B.R.: The impact of information technology infrastructure flexibility on strategic alignment and applications implementation. In: Communications of the AIS (11) 2003, pp. 191-206.

Chwelos, P., Benbasat, I., and Dexter, A.: Research report: empirical test of an EDI adoption model. In: Information Systems Research (12:3) 2001, pp. 304-321.

Cooper, A.C., and Zmud, R.W.: Information technology implementation research: a technological diffusion approach. In: Management Science (36:2) 1990, pp. 123-139.

Daft, R.L.: A Dual-Core Model of Organizational Innovation. In: The Academy of Management Journal (21:2), June 1978, p. 193.210.

DiMaggio, P.J., and Powell, W.W.: The Iron Cage Revisited: Institutional Isomorphism and Collective Rationality in Organizational Fields. In: American Sociological Review (48:2) 1983, pp. 147-160.

Evans, J.S.: Strategic Flexibility for High Technology Manoeuvres: A Conceptual Framework. In: Journal of Management Studies (28:1) 1991, pp. 69-89.

Fichman, R.G.: Going Beyond the Dominant Paradigm for Information Technology Innovation Research: Emerging Concepts and Methods. In: Journal of the Association for Information Systems (5:8), August 2004, pp. 314-355.

Frambach, R.T., and Schillewaert, N.: Organizational innovation adoption - A multi-level framework of determinants and opportunities for future research. In: Journal of Business Research (55:2) 2002, pp. 163-176.

Gallivan, M.J.: Organizational adoption and assimilation of complex technological innovations: development and application of a new framework. In: The DATA BASE for Advances in Information Systems (32:3) 2001, pp. 51-85.

Galunic, D.C., and Rodan, S.: Resource recombinations in the firm: knowledge structures and the potential for Schumpeterian innovation. In: Strategic Management Journal (19:12) 1998, pp. 1193-1201.

Goles, T., and Chin, W.W.: Information systems outsourcing relationship factors: detailed conceptualization and initial evidence. In: The DATA BASE for Advances in Information Systems (36:4) 2005, pp. 47-67.

Hansen, M.T.: The search-transfer problem: the role of weak ties in sharing knowledge across organization subunits. In: Administrative Science Quarterly (44:1) 1999, pp. 82-111.

Henderson, B.D., and Venkatraman, N.: Strategic alignment: leveraging information technology for transforming organizations. In: IBM Systems Journal (32:1) 1993, pp. 4-16.

Henderson, J.C., and Sifonis, J.G.: The Value of Strategic IS Planning: Understanding Consistency, Validity, and IS Markets. In: MIS Quarterly (12:2) 1988, p. 186.

Iacovou, C.L., Benbasat, I., and Dexter, A.S.: Electronic data interchange and small organizations: Adoption and impact of technology. In: MIS Quarterly (19:4) 1995, pp. 465-485.

Jeyaraj, A., Rottman, J.W., and Lacity, M.C.: A review of the predictors, linkages, and biases in IT innovation adoption research. In: Journal of Information Technology (21) 2006, pp. 1-23.

Kantor, R.M.: When Giants Learn to Dance: Mastering the Challenge of Strategy, Management and Careers in the 1990s. Simon and Schuster, New York, 1994, (as of).

Kearns, G.S., and Lederer, A.L.: A Resource-Based View of Strategic IT Alignment: How Knowledge Sharing Creates Competitive Advantage. In: Decision Sciences (34:1) 2003, pp. 1-29.

Kessler, E.H.: Organizational innovation: A multi-level decision-theoretic perspective. In: International Journal of Innovation Management (8:3) 2004, p. 275.

Khalifa, M., and Davison, R.M.: SME Adoption of IT: The Case of Electronic Trading Systems. In: IEEE Transactions on Engineering Management (53:2), May 2006, pp. 275-284.

Klein, K.J., and Sorra, J.S.: The challenge of innovation implementation. In: Academy of Management Review (21:4) 1996, p. 1055.

Kuan, K.K.Y., and Chau, P.Y.K.: A perception-based model for EDI adoption in small businesses using a technology-organization-environment framework. In: Information and Management (38) 2001, pp. 507-521.

Lederer, A.L., and Burky, L.B.: Understanding top management's objectives: a management information systems concern. In: Journal of Information Systems (3:1) 1989, pp. 49-66.

Lederer, A.L., and Mendelow, A.L.: Information resource planning: overcoming difficulties in identifying top management's objectives. In: MIS Quarterly (11:3) 1987, pp. 389-399.

Lederer, A.L., and Mendelow, A.L.: Coordination of information systems plans with business plans. In: Journal of Management Information Systems (6:2) 1989, pp. 5-19.

Loh, L., and Venkatraman, N.: Diffusion of IT outsourcing: influence sources and the Kodak effect. In: Information Systems Research (3:4) 1992, pp. 334-358.

Luftman, J.: Assessing business-IT alignment maturity. In: Communications of the AIS (4:14) 2000, pp. 1-50.

Luftman, J., Papp, R., and Bries, T.: Enablers and inhibitors of Business-IT alignment. In: Communications of the AIS (1) 1999, pp. 1-33.

Meyer, J., and Rowan, B.: Institutionalized organizations: Formal structure as myth and ceremony. In: American Journal of Sociology (83:2) 1977, pp. 340-363.

Mingers, J.: Combining IS Research Methods: Towards a Pluralist Methodology. In: Information Systems Research (12:3) 2001, pp. 240-259.

Nelson, K.M., and Cooprider, J.G.: The contribution of shared knowledge to IS group performance. In: MIS Quarterly (20:4) 1996, pp. 409-432.

Papp, R.: Business-IT alignment: productivity paradoy payoff? In: Industrial Management & Data Systems (99:8) 1999, pp. 367-373.

Plouffe, C.R., Hulland, J.S., and Vandenbosch, M.: Research Report: Richness Versus Parsimony in Modeling Technology Adoption Decisions-- Understanding Merchant Adoption of a Smart Card-Based Payment System. In: Information Systems Research (12:2) 2001, p. 208.

Powell, T.C., and Dent-Micallef, A.: Information Technology as Competitive Advantage: The Role of Human, Business, and Technology Resources. In: Strategic Management Journal (18:5) 1997, pp. 375-405.

Ramamurthy, K.: Moderating influences of organizational attitude and compatibility on implementation success from computer-integrated manufacturing technology. In: International Journal of Production Research (32:10) 1994, pp. 2251-2273.

Reich, B.H., and Benbasat, I.: Measuring the linkage between business and information technology objectives. In: MIS Quarterly (20:1) 1996, pp. 55-81.

Reich, B.H., and Benbasat, I.: Factors that influence the social dimension of alignment between business and information technology objectives. In: MIS Quarterly (24:1) 2000, pp. 81-113.

Sabherwal, R., and Chan, Y.E.: Alignment between business and IS strategies: a study of prospectors, analyzers, and defenders. In: Information Systems Research (12:1) 2001, pp. 11-33.

Sambamurthy, V., and Zmud, R.W.: At the heart of success: organization-wide management competencies. In: Steps to the future: fresh thinking on the management of IT-based organizational transformation, C. Sauer and P. Yetton (eds.), Jossey-Bass Publishers, San Francisco (CA), 1997, pp. 143-163.

Sambamurthy, V., and Zmud, R.W.: Arrangements for information technology governance: a theory of multiple contingencies. In: MIS Quarterly (23:2) 1999, pp. 261-290.

Saunders, C.S., and Clark, S.: EDI adoption and implementation: A focus on inter-organizational linkages. In: Information Resource Management Journal (5:1) 1992, pp. 9-19.

Scott, W.R.: Institutions and Organizations. Sage Publications, 2001.

Tallon, P.P., Kraemer, K.L., and Gurbaxani, V.: Executives' Perceptions of the Business Value of Information Technology: A Process-Oriented Approach. In: Journal of Management Information Systems (16:4) 2000a, pp. 145-173.

Tallon, P.P., Kreamer, K.L., and Gurbaxani, V.: Executives perception of the business value of information technology: a process-oriented approach. In: Journal of Management Information Systems (16:4) 2000b, pp. 145-173.

Teo, H.H., Wei, K.K., and Benbasat, I.: Predicting intention to adopt interorganizational linkages: an institutional perspective. In: MIS Quarterly (27:1) 2003, pp. 19-49.

Teo, T.S.H., and King, W.R.: Assessing the impact of integrating business planning and IS planning. In: Information & Management (30:6) 1996, pp. 309-321.

Tiwana, A., Bharadwaj, A., and Sambamurthy, V.: The antecedents of information systems development capability in firms: a knowledge integration perspective. 24th International Conference on Information Systems (ICIS), Seattle (WA), USA, 2003, pp. 246-258.

Venkatraman, N., and Ramanujam, V.: Measurement of business economic performance: an examination of method convergence. In: Journal of Management (13:1) 1987, pp. 109-122.

Wagner, H.-T.: A Resource-based Perspective on IT Business Alignment and Performance - Theoretical Foundation and Empirical Evidence. Doctoral Dissertation, Goethe University, Frankfurt am Main, 2006.

Wagner, H.-T., and Weitzel, T.: Modeling the impact of alignment routines on IT performance: an approach to making the resource based view explicit. 38th Hawaii International Conference on System Sciences (HICSS-38), Waikoloa, HI, USA, 2005.

Wagner, H.-T., and Weitzel, T.: Operational IT Business Alignment as the Missing Link from IT Strategy to Firm Success. 12th Americas Conference on Information Systems (AMCIS 2006), Acapulco, Mexico, 2006.

Zmud, R.W.: Building relationships throughout the corporate entity. In: Transforming the IT organization: thhe mission, the framework, the transition, J. Elam, M. Ginzberg, P. Keen and R.W. Zmud (eds.), 1988, Washington, 1988, pp. 55-82

Organizational Readiness for Business Process Outsourcing: A Model of Determinants and Impact on Outsourcing Success[1]

Sebastian F. Martin	Daniel Beimborn
E-Finance Lab	E-Finance Lab
Institute for Information Systems	Institute for Information Systems
Goethe University, Frankfurt,	Goethe University, Frankfurt,
Germany	Germany
smartin@wiwi.uni-frankfurt.de	beimborn@wiwi.uni-frankfurt.de
Mihir A. Parikh	Tim Weitzel
College of Business Administration	Chair of Information Systems
University of Central Florida, USA	Bamberg University, Germany
mihir.parikh@bus.ucf.edu	tweitzel@wiwi.uni-frankfurt.de

Abstract

In innovation adoption literature, the important role of the organizational context as a determinant of information systems (IS) success has long been pointed out. Various factors such as top management support, process formalization, and availability of resources have been shown to contribute to the successful implementation of new information systems. By drawing on relevant insights from IT innovations literature, our conceptual piece of research aims at identifying organizational context factors which are critical for the success of business process outsourcing (BPO) as part of a firm's overall Business Process Management activities. More specifically, process readiness, IT readiness and business management readiness are proposed to be important dimensions of organizational readiness for BPO. Furthermore, IT business alignment, as a

---

[1] This paper has been published in the Proceedings of the Hawaii International Conference on System Sciences (HICSS-41), Big Island, Hawaii, USA, 20d08

routine-based process of knowledge sharing and creation, is proposed to be a driver of organizational readiness for BPO.

1 Introduction

Business Process Management (BPM) is increasingly attracting interests of both practitioners and researchers, as it promises to improve business agility and operational governance by discovering, analyzing, modeling, simulating, optimizing, executing and governing business processes using well-defined methods, policies, metrics, practices, and software tools. Despite its relative recentness, business process outsourcing (BPO) is emerging to be one of the most promising instruments of BPM that optimizes performance in both core and non-core business processes. It aims to develop mutually beneficial interorganizational alliances among firms based on the level of competence in various business processes. The emergence of standardized and open IT platforms in recent years has made such alliances not only operationally feasible but also economically attractive.

Nevertheless, until now BPO has received little attention in academic literature (Rouse et al. 2004). Moreover, descriptive studies found a significant number of BPO deals showing serious problems; a survey (Wahrenburg et al. 2005) conducted in 2004 among Germany's 500 largest banks on process performance issues, the role of IT, and outsourcing tendencies in the credit business found that among the managers of banks which had already outsourced (parts of) their credit process, practically no one was fully contented with the outcomes of the outsourcing deal. Only 29% of the managers in charge with the specific process stated to be "rather content" with the outcomes of BPO. A subsequent study found that the risk of *not achieving expected cost savings* from an outsourcing deal (because the underlying business case does not contain all prospective costs) ranged among the top three managerial concerns regarding business process outsourcing (BPO) (Wüllenweber et al. 2006).

Much of the academic literature on outsourcing focuses on the outcomes of outsourcing (Dibbern et al. 2004). The general tenor is that customers can successfully exploit the outsourcing market, but that it requires a tremendous amount of in-house management (Lacity et al. 2003). But while some researchers have focused on the impact of contract design and relationship quality between outsourcer and service provider, only a few papers have addressed the organizational context – i.e., factors grounded within the outsourcer's organization – as a determinant of successful outsourcing.

By contrast, the literature strand on the adoption and implementation of IT innovations by organizations has pointed out the important role of the organizational context as a determinant of successful innovation adoption and implementation for a long time (Raymond 1990). It has been stressed that firms need to become organizationally ready in order to successfully adopt and implement an (IT) innovation (Snyder-Halpern 2001).

When outsourcing IT-intense processes – such as credit processing or other transactional or back-office processes in the financial services industry, the outsourcer's IT unit needs to provide strong support to the business domain – for example, by helping managers to identify potential hyphenation points where the business process can be split between the outsourcer and the sourcing provider, by determining prospective costs of systems integration, and by interfacing the IT applications supporting the business process. From a knowledge-theoretical point of view, this means that different knowledge pools within the organization – namely, the IT and business units – need to be incorporated into the process of BPO adoption. IT and business units need to work together in an aligned way.

The objective of this ongoing study is twofold. First, by drawing on insights from innovation adoption literature we want to explore relevant dimensions of organizational readiness for BPO and to evaluate their impact on BPO success. Second, we want to assess the role of IT business alignment as a determinant of organizational BPO readiness. The purpose is to enhance our understanding of nuances of BPM by assessing the impact of the strength of relationship among business processes, practices and coordination of the business and IT sides of a firm on the firm's readiness at three levels to carry out this emerging BPM practice.

In this context, we will specifically address both, the business knowledge of IT managers (which has been typically considered in most of the past alignment research) as well as the IT knowledge of business managers (which has been widely ignored so far).

The research questions motivating this project thus are:

1. What are relevant dimensions of organizational readiness for BPO and what is their impact on BPO success?

2. What is the impact of IT business alignment on the achievement of organizational readiness for BPO?

2 Theoretical Foundation

2.1 Business Process Outsourcing

BPO has only recently attracted the attention of researchers although it has been acknowledged in the past to be one of the largest areas of growth in the outsourcing market (Gartner Group 2004). BPO is generally seen as the delegation of entire, or parts of, organizational business processes to a third party provider – including the hardware and software that supports those processes (Rouse et al. 2004; Willcocks et al. 2004). BPO thus represents a combination of traditional information technology outsourcing (ITO), which has been a major trend since the early 1990s (Dibbern et al. 2004), and the outsourcing of non-IS business functions (Kakabadse et al. 2002). At the same time, BPO is orthogonal to the concept of ITO since it does not separate the tight interconnection between business unit and IT unit. Nevertheless, we argue that this interconnection has a potential impact on successful BPO because outsourcing IT-intense parts of the firm requires the subsequent implementation of inter-organizational systems to ensure straight-through processing. Thus, a strong involvement of the IT organization throughout the process of outsourcing is required.

BPO represents a *major administrative innovation* for today's organizations, very similar to how IT outsourcing represented a fundamental change for the way organizations could meet their IT needs in the early 1990s (Loh et al. 1992). This perspective allows us to base our research efforts on prior findings from the literature on organizational adoption of innovations, which thus provides a suitable theoretical basis for analyzing the adoption of BPO by organizations.

2.2 Organizational Readiness

As we already mentioned, the role of the organizational context as an important determinant of successful innovation adoption and implementation has been pointed out for a long time. Various factors such as firm size, process formalization, and resources have been shown to contribute to the successful implementation of information systems (Ein-Dor et al. 1978; Raymond 1990).

The notion of organizational readiness has been described in innovation literature as the level of preparedness of a firm for adopting and implementing an (IT) innovation (Iacovou et al. 1995). This literature postulates that organizational innovation readiness – in terms of a sophisticated IT, integrated processes, availability of slack resources and the like – help to lower the level of risk associated with the innovation and thus contributes to more successful innovation outcomes (Snyder et al. 2006). Furthermore, it speculates that a managerial lack of information about the own organizational innovation readiness comes along with increased uncertainty about the risks posed by the innovation and thus with a decreased ability to mitigate those risks (Snyder-Halpern 2001).

However, while the importance of organizational readiness for successful innovation adoption and implementation has been highlighted repeatedly, there is no consensus about which dimensions constitute organizational readiness. In Iacovou et al.'s model of EDI adoption by small and mid-sized enterprises, organizational readiness refers to the *level of financial resources* and *availability and sophistication of the technological resources* of the firm (Iacovou et al. 1995). The availability of resources is considered to be important because "small firms tend to lack the resources that are necessary for EDI and other IT investments" (Iacovou et al. 1995). Chang et al. (Chang et al. 2005) extend the scope of organizational readiness by including *process integration* as a further measure for the preparedness of a firm to adopt IT innovations. Furthermore, the *process readiness* dimension has been defined as the "level of fit" between the existing business processes within the adopting firm and the prospective innovation (Snyder-Halpern 2001). This "level of fit" reflects the extent to which processes and the innovation need to be altered in order to be compatible to each other (Snyder-Halpern 2001). Researchers also noted the importance of *inner-organizational business process integration* for the successful adoption of IOS, positing that firms with a high degree of integration within their business processes are better prepared to undertake cooperation projects by means of IOS (Chang et al. 2005; Iacovou et al. 1995).

In this paper, we develop a concept of organizational readiness for BPO by drawing on the insights from innovation literature about the organizational factors which contribute to the successful adoption of innovations. Hereby, we concentrate on the organizational context from an *outsourcer's perspective*.

2.3 IT Business Alignment

As mentioned in the introduction, IT and business units need to work together in an aligned way throughout the whole process of BPO implementation. This is why we regard IT business alignment as an important factor for achieving high organizational readiness for BPO.

There is an ongoing discussion about whether alignment should be regarded as a state (an outcome) or as a process which affects the outcome dimensions (Sabherwal et al. 2001a). Several authors link alignment to the resource-based view and describe it as a dynamic capability to develop and implement congruent IT and business plans (e.g., Sambamurthy et al. 1999; Wagner et al. 2005). The most prominent argument for the view of alignment as a process stems from Kearns and Lederer who state that alignment is a "process in which managers participate in the exchange of knowledge" (Kearns et al. 2003). The alignment process itself is based on the concept of routines which describe the formal and informal purposeful interaction of entities within an organization (Amit et al. 1993). Routines are essentially patterns of activity based on human actors (Wagner 2007). "Smoothly functioning routines between IT and business units are seen as valuable, leading to a more effective development and use of IT" (Wagner et al. 2005).

Prior research has identified two primary consequences of alignment: increased IS effectiveness (Chan et al. 1997) and increased firm performance (Sabherwal et al. 2001a). In contrast, misalignment of business and IT has been said to lead to undesirable organizational effects like poor utilization of scarce organizational resources, sub-optimal performance of business units and the organization, a cyclical relationship between higher IS spending and expectations for success, costly IS investments with low yield returns, missed identification of high potential IS applications, and lack of capitalization of first-rate technology-related ideas (Chan 2002; Lederer et al. 1987).

In this paper, we argue that the process of IT business alignment, based on smoothly functioning communication routines, is an important prerequisite for the achievement of high organizational readiness for BPO.

3 Research Model and Propositions

Based on a literature review, we consider three factors as essential dimensions of organizational readiness for BPO. Our main propositions are that these factors are drivers for BPO success and that they are in turn driven by the smooth alignment process between IT and business organizations of the outsourcing firm. These relationships are summarized in Figure 1.

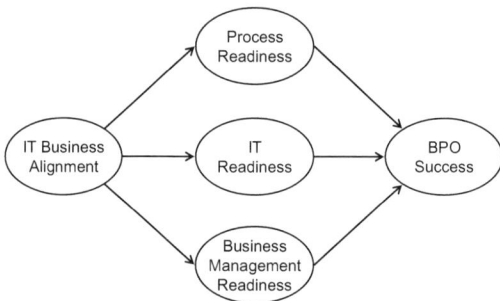

Figure 1: Proposed Research Model

Obviously, business process-oriented research models highly depend on the characteristics of the particular business process to be analyzed. Although we develop a generic model, we are aware of this and will consider several process characteristics, discussed by the literature, such as variety (Collier et al. 1998; Kellog et al. 1995; Schmenner 2004; Tinnila et al. 1995), customer interaction and influence (Buzacott 2000; Ding et al. 2007; Silvestro et al. 1992), degree of automation, complexity (Shostack 1987), flexibility (Heim et al. 2001), and information intensity (Krcmar 2005), as control variables for the overall model. This allows us to evaluate the following constructs in light of specific process requirements in different industries and business segments. Additionally, we would like to point out the four propositions – P1, P2, P3 and P4 – that directly relate to BPM as they are aimed at a firm's readiness to undertake a specific process management initiative and the likelihood of success in that initiative.

Whereas, the other two propositions – P5 and P6 – provide insights on the overall readiness of the firm's business and IT sides for undertaking any interorganizational process management initiative.

3.1 BPO Success

Many researchers have conducted studies on outsourcing success without producing a common definition of what exactly constitutes outsourcing success (Dibbern et al. 2004). Lacity et al. (Lacity et al. 1996) have found that the *achievement of anticipated cost savings* was the criterion used by most companies when assessing outsourcing success. Therefore, based on Lacity et al., we use the achievement of targeted cost savings as the measure for BPO success.

3.2 Process Readiness

When deciding to alter a business process by outsourcing (parts of) it, the implications or consequences of this action need to be well comprehended by the managers in charge. Many authors have stressed the importance of a firm's business processes being prepared for the adoption and implementation of an innovation (Chang et al. 2005; Iacovou et al. 1995; Premkumar et al. 1995). Raymond (Raymond 1990) posits that "formalization requires that organizational processes be well understood, if explicit procedures, instructions, and communications are to govern them". Ein-Dor and Segev (Ein-Dor et al. 1978) proposed that organizations with a high degree of process formalization were more likely to successfully adopt and implement an innovation. In the domain of BPO, altering the process by splitting it up between two organizations *represents* the innovation. This underlines the importance that the outsourcer thoroughly understands the implications, or side effects, of BPO implementation. Managers need to understand to what extent, and in which ways, altering a process by outsourcing (parts of) it, affects the other processes which are to be kept in-house. Being able to foresee all relevant side effects of

BPO necessitates a thorough understanding of the process subject to outsourcing and of its interfaces to the surrounding processes. We therefore conceptualize process readiness for BPO as the *degree of formalization* of the processes subject to BPO, reflected by the existence of documentation, rules, procedures, and clear management practices (Ein-Dor et al. 1978).

It has been shown that process formalization is related to more efficiency, involving the application of rules and standard procedures to reduce ambiguity (Dewett et al. 2001). Thus, we expect that high levels of process formalization will lead to more efficiency and less ambiguity during the process of BPO implementation, helping to avoid unexpected costs and thus to achieve anticipated cost savings. Therefore, we propose that

P1 Higher levels of process readiness lead to higher levels of BPO success.

3.3 IT Readiness

Based on Byrd and Turner (Byrd et al. 2000), Duncan (Duncan 1995), and Bassellier and Benbasat (Bassellier et al. 2004), we conceptualize IT readiness as the level of flexibility of the outsourcing organization's IT infrastructure and the business knowledge of IT managers.

Prior research divides IT infrastructure into two components (Byrd et al. 2000; Duncan 1995): technical IT infrastructure and human IT infrastructure. The technical infrastructure is referred to as "set of shared, tangible IT resources forming a foundation for business applications" (Byrd et al. 2000). The human IT infrastructure refers to the *technology management* knowledge and skills and *technical* knowledge and skills of the IT personnel (Lee et al. 1995). Duncan (Duncan 1995) states that "infrastructure is flexible as the IT organization is able to respond rapidly and effectively to emergent needs or opportunities".

Byrd and Turner (Byrd et al. 2001) state that a flexible IT infrastructure can "support the design, development, and implementation of a heterogeneity of business applications. [...] For example, if an organization supports a wide variety of hardware and software, that organization can more easily cope with changes [...]". In the context of BPO, we expect a high degree of IT readiness to require *fewer investments in IT systems and IT expertise*, thus lowering the costs of BPO implementation and helping to achieve the targeted cost savings.

Dimensions	Description	Sources
Process Readiness - Process formalization	• Degree of process formalization indicated by the existence of rules, procedures, and clear management practices for the processes affected by BPO	(Ein-Dor et al. 1978), (Raymond 1990)
IT Readiness - IT infrastructure flexibility - Business knowledge of IT managers	• Technical IT infrastructure as the "set of shared, tangible IT resources forming a foundation for business applications". • Human IT infrastructure as the technology management knowledge and skills and technical knowledge and skills of the IT personnel. • Knowledge and skills of IT professionals that enable them to "understand the business domain, speak the language of business, and interact with their business partners"	(Bassellier et al. 2004), (Byrd et al. 2000), (Byrd et al. 2001), (Duncan 1995)
Business Management Readiness - IT knowledge of business managers - Experienced project leader - Top management support	• Experience and knowledge of business managers that enables them to exert IT leadership in their area of business. • Active support by top managers for the BPO implementation project	(Bassellier 2001), (Jeyaraj et al. 2006), (Snyder-Halpern 2001)

Table 1: Dimensions of organizational readiness for BPO

Bassellier and Benbasat (Bassellier et al. 2004) found that IT professionals have a greater intention to develop and strengthen relationships with the business organization when they reach higher levels of business competence. They define business competence of IT managers as "the set of business and interpersonal knowledge and skills possessed by IT professionals that enable them to understand the business domain, speak the language of business, and interact with their business partners" (Bassellier et al. 2004). Relationships between business and IT are seen as essential for achieving high performance from IT (Peppard et al. 1999; Wagner 2007). It was also discussed that a lack of business knowledge of IT managers leads to an inaccurate understanding of the actual requirements (Nelson et al. 1996). We conclude that, for BPO implementation, higher business competence of IT managers leads to a better understanding of the requirements posed by BPO to the IT domain and therefore to a more efficient and effective execution of IT-related tasks during BPO implementation (like interfacing IT applications and creating user interfaces).

Therefore, we propose:

P2 Higher levels of IT readiness lead to higher levels of BPO success.

3.4 Business Management Readiness

While IT readiness describes the IT context within the outsourcing firm, business management readiness refers to the fostering factors for BPO grounded within the outsourcer's business domain. One important aspect of business management readiness discussed in prior literature is the *experience of business managers* with outsourcing projects (Snyder-Halpern 2001). The underlying premise here is that organizations are able to learn from their experiences and that learning is a means of coping with change (Senge 1990). Furthermore, *top management support* has been widely acknowledged as one of the most important stimuli for successful innovation adoption (Jeyaraj et al. 2006). It seems logical to conclude that for BPO, too, the availability of an experienced project leader and active support from top management are important factors for the implementation of BPO within time and budget, thus helping to achieve targeted cost savings from BPO.

As mentioned earlier, the outsourcing of IT-intense business processes typically has strong IT implications, namely the need to interface IT applications supporting the business process with other internal and external systems. The business problem, then, is how to best manage the interorganizational context from an IT perspective. Lack of attention to integrating information systems has been identified as one of the main reasons for failure of interorganizational projects (Mehta et al. 2007). As stated earlier, IT innovation literature mentions that knowledge of managers about their own organizational readiness fosters their ability to understand and mitigate the risks posed by the adoption of an innovation (Snyder-Halpern 2001; Zaltman et al. 1973). Bassellier et al. (Bassellier 2001) pointed out the importance of business managers' IT competence for their ability to exert IT leadership in their area of business:

"Business managers are now expected to deploy IT effectively and strategically, to assume ownership of IT projects within their domain of business responsibility, to develop a partnership with IT professionals, and to take the leadership in IT implementation" (Bassellier 2001). We argue that in the domain of BPO, IT competence enables business managers to understand the IT-related challenges posed by BPO and to cope with those challenges by taking the "right" business decisions. Therefore, IT competence of business managers helps to avoid unexpected costs and to achieve anticipated savings. We thus propose:

P3 Higher levels of business management readiness lead to higher levels of BPO success.

3.5 IT Business Alignment

In this article, we explicitly draw upon the *process view* of alignment, as described earlier. We regard alignment as a continuous process of communication and knowledge sharing, based on routines as the underlying dynamic element. According to Hansen (Hansen 2002), knowledge sharing among people from different subunits is a dual problem of searching for (looking for and identifying) and transferring (moving and incorporating) knowledge across organizational (sub)units.

In this view, alignment describes effective communication and knowledge exchange patterns which affect the outcome dimensions of shared knowledge and mutual understanding (Reich et al. 2000; Tiwana et al. 2003) and lead to the fit of business and IT strategies and plans (Bergeron et al. 2004). Nelson and Winter (Nelson et al. 1982) refer to such exchange patterns as "routines" which are to the organization what skills are to the individual, incorporating tacit knowledge and unconscious coordination (Wagner et al. 2005).

Prior research has stated that high degrees of process formalization and strong alignment routines may also lead to more inertia and thus to *less* organizational flexibility (Sabherwal et al. 2001b; Wagner 2007). The argument here is that a high level of alignment and strong process formalization may reduce the recognition of a possible need for change, thus reducing flexibility (Wagner 2007). For this debate it is important to keep in mind that the concept of organizational flexibility has two temporal aspects, which comprise "an ex ante mode – preparing in advance for some future transformation, and an ex post mode – after-the-fact adjustments undertaken once a triggering episode has occurred" (Evans 1991). While alignment may reduce a firm's ability to *recognize* the need for change (ex ante), we argue that ex post – i.e., once the need for change has been recognized – good alignment will act as a driver for efficient adaptation of the firm, because routine frequent interaction and knowledge sharing increase the ability of individuals from different units to know where to find and get knowledge from diverse parties (Wagner et al. 2006). This assumption is supported by Beimborn et al. (Beimborn et al. 2006) who found a strong positive link between operational alignment and IT flexibility of a firm, because of increasing business knowledge availability to the IT domain through knowledge exchange routines.

Prior research has also discussed the link between IT business alignment and organizational maturity, which is the degree to which organizational processes have been systemized by rules, procedures, and organizational practices (Raymond 1990). It has been stated that communication and regular knowledge exchange lead to a better understanding of business processes and of the underlying IT and thus to higher organizational maturity (Wagner 2007).

Based on these findings, we thus conclude that routine-based, frequent interaction between business and IT domain also leads to a higher IT understanding of business managers, which in turn helps them to recognize and mitigate IT-related risks of BPO. We thus postulate that strong IT business alignment processes lead to high organizational readiness for BPO. More specifically:

P4 By enhancing organizational maturity, strong IT business alignment leads to higher process readiness for BPO.

P5 By enhancing IT flexibility and business knowledge of IT managers, strong IT business alignment leads to higher IT readiness.

P6 By enhancing business managers' understanding of IT, alignment leads to higher business management readiness.

4 Proposed Research Approach and Unit of Analysis

This section gives a brief overview on the research approach and the unit of analysis.

This research project consists of three phases. Phase 1 (of which the current paper is a first result) is a piece of descriptive research. The aim of this phase was to identify and narrow down the problem to be studied (which arises from the poor outcomes of BPO in the German banking sector). We identified and formulated relevant research questions for this problem domain, stated our intended contribution to practice and theory, developed a theory-based research model and, based on this model, formulated the expected results of the study.

Phases 2 and 3 will consist of a qualitative and a quantitative research step, respectively. Since the constructs of the research model and most of the hypotheses are already well grounded in theory, the appropriate research paradigm is positivism. Nevertheless, within the positivist context we want to get deeper insights into what the relevant facets of the chosen constructs in the relevant context of BPO adoption are and therefore propose a sequential data collection process of both case studies and a subsequent quantitative approach based on the case study results. Applying such dual approaches in IS research is asked for by Mingers (2001), who found that only a small minority of all empirical research works applied more than one research method. Since case study research has been accepted as a valid and valuable research approach within the positivist paradigm (Benbasat et al. 1987; Iivari 1991; Lee 1989), the combination of both approaches for data collection and analysis allows to deeper focus on specific aspects of reality and thereby getting a richer understanding of the object of analysis. For the aim of this research we intend to conduct a multiple case study since variability of the main construct – alignment – is needed. To reduce the impact of further organizational factors which might affect the analysis, we will conduct the case studies in a rather homogenous industry (in terms of product variety).

An evolving trend of outsourcing parts of the back office of the mortgage business to so-called credit factories may currently be observed in the German banking industry. To be able to offer mortgage products in an effective manner, the front office needs to get very prompt feedback from the evaluation (pre-defined scoring provided by the sourcing provider) after the credit application data has been entered. After granting the loan, the electronic credit file is set up and archived by the credit factory. In cases of customer contact (e.g. if the customer situation changes or the loan has to be prolonged), the electronic credit file is handed over to the bank. These patterns just represent some examples of bank-credit factory interaction, but they reveal that tight integration of the bank's systems with the applications of the service provider has to be established.

The banking industry in Germany is highly regulated and consists of three different sectors. Two of them, the public savings bank sector and the credit cooperative sector, internally consist of autonomous, but structurally quite similar institutions (similar owner structure, quite similar product portfolio, often they even use the same software provided by a joint data processing center). Banks of these sectors provide, together with the increasing dynamics of the BPO market, a promising homogenous data base for conducting multiple case studies on the same phenomenon in different but structurally similar firms. This enables us to discard many disturbing factors (Eisenhardt 1989; Yin 2002).

The case studies are intended to give valuable insights for the design of the subsequent quantitative data collection step (phase 3). Since BPO of mortgage processing is a starting trend in Germany, there comes up the opportunity of examining BPO success and the underlying alignment dimensions to validate case study findings on a cross-sectional basis. Moreover, the survey can be extended to other – more mature – BPO segments in the financial services industry, such as payments processing, securities processing, or custody and account management, in order to take into account different process characteristics which might affect the results and therefore have to be considered as control variables as proposed at the beginning of section 3. Those differ in degree of technical integration and type of IOS (and therefore may have differing demands towards IT business alignment), but also are embedded in the quite homogenous and regulated banking industry to allow comparisons and to make a step towards the generalizability of the results.

5 Conclusion

Many firms are considering outsourcing some of their business processes under their overall business process management (BPM) programs. An attractive argument for such practice is that BPO enables firms to achieve a very high degree of process efficiencies and effectiveness through the economies of scale and scope offered by external business process providers. However, being a recent phenomenon, success factors in BPO are not well understood. It is unclear why some firms do not achieve the same degree of success as others do in their BPO initiatives causing overall failure or even negative effects in their BPM programs. In this paper, we developed a research model that captures the effect of organizational readiness on BPO success as well as the enabling effect of alignment for organizational readiness. The three dimensions of organizational readiness, i.e. process readiness, IT readiness and business management readiness, are limited to *readiness for BPO* as a specific type of interorganizational relationship involving a process management initiative. While restricting the meaning of this notion, this limitation may at the same time be considered a strength of our research because it will allow us to clearly pinpoint the dimensions of this notion within this narrow focus.

This model and the subsequent empirical validation will enhance our understanding of the organizational factors that affect successful outsourcing of business processes by integrating findings from the adoption of innovations stream of research with findings from the outsourcing and the IT business alignment literature. To our knowledge, this paper is one of the first to specifically address not only business knowledge of IT managers as a means for achieving alignment, but also IT knowledge of business managers, thus acknowledging that alignment may be built from both sides, not just from IT side.

The use of proxy variables (namely, the achievement of targeted cost savings) for measuring outsourcing success may be viewed as another limitation of this research. Nevertheless, the use of proxy variables is a widely-spread practice when direct measures for the construct of interest are missing. As a further limitation, we need to state that we are aware of the existence of a principal-agent problem in the context of BPO. Good IT business alignment may under certain circumstances negatively impact outsourcing success – namely, if IT and business managers fear personal negative consequences of some sort from BPO (for example, loss of power or even losing their jobs). If both agree that successful BPO implementation will lead to personal disadvantages for themselves, they may work together seeking to bring the deal to failure. In the empirical part of the project, we will need to explicitly check for this effect by asking if IT and business managers have been given personal incentives to perform well in implementing BPO.

6 Acknowledgement

This work was developed as part of a research project of the E-Finance Lab, Frankfurt am Main, Germany (www.efinancelab.com). We are indebted to the participating universities and industry partners.

7 References

Amit, R., and Schoemaker, P. "Strategic assets and organizational rent," *Strategic Management Journal* (14:1) 1993, pp 33-46.

Bassellier, G. "Information Technology Competence of Business Managers: A Definition and Research Model," *Journal of Management Information Systems* (17:4) 2001, pp 159-182.

Bassellier, G., and Benbasat, I. "Business Competence of Information Technology Professionals: Conceptual Development and Influence on IT-Business Partnerships," *MIS Quarterly* (28:4) 2004, pp 673-694.

Beimborn, D., Franke, J., Wagner, H.-T., and Weitzel, T. "Strategy matters - The role of strategy type for IT business value," 12th Americas Conference on Information Systems (AMCIS), Acapulco, Mexico, 2006.

Benbasat, I., Goldstein, D.K., and Mead, M. "The Case Research Strategy in Studies of Information Systems," *MIS Quarterly* (11:3) 1987, pp 369-386.

Bergeron, F., Raymond, L., and Rivard, S. "Ideal patterns of strategic alignment and business performance," *Information & Management* (41:8) 2004, pp 1003-1020.

Buzacott, J.A. "Service System Structure," *International Journal of Production Economics* (68:1) 2000, pp 15-27.

Byrd, T.A., and Turner, D.E. "Measuring the flexibility of information technology infrastructure: exploratory analysis of a construct," *Journal of Management Information Systems* (17:1) 2000, pp 167-208.

Byrd, T.A., and Turner, D.E. "An exploratory examination of the relationship between flexible IT infrastructure and competitive advantage," *Information and Management* (39:1) 2001, pp 41-52.

Chan, Y.E. "Why haven't we mastered alignment? The importance of the informal organization structure," *MIS Quarterly Executive* (1:2) 2002, pp 97-112.

Chan, Y.E., Huff, A.S., Barclay, D.W., and Copeland, D.G. "Business strategic orientation, information systems strategic orientation, and strategic alignment," *Information Systems Research* (8:2) 1997, pp 125-150.

Chang, H.L., and Chen, S.H. "Assessing the Readiness of Internet-Based IOS and Evaluating Its Impact on Adoption," *System Sciences, 2005. HICSS'05. Proceedings of the 38th Annual Hawaii International Conference on*) 2005, pp 207b-207b.

Collier, D.A., and Meyer, S.M. "A Service Positioning Matrix," *International Journal of Operations & Production Management* (18:12) 1998, pp 1223-1244.

Dewett, T., and Jones, G.R. "The role of information technology in the organization: a review, model, and assessment," *Journal of Management* (27:3) 2001, p 313.

Dibbern, J., Goles, T., Hirschheim, R., and Jayatilaka, B. "Information systems outsourcing: a survey and analysis of the literature," *The DATA BASE for Advantages in Information Systems* (35:4) 2004, pp 6-102.

Ding, X., Verma, R., and Iqbal, Z. "Self-Service Technology and Online Financial Service Choice," *International Journal of Service Industry Management* (18:3) 2007, pp 246-268.

Duncan, N.B. "Capturing flexibility of information technology infrastructure: a study of resource characteristics and their measure," *Journal of Management Information Systems* (12:2) 1995, pp 37-57.

Ein-Dor, P., and Segev, E. "Organizational context and the success of management information systems," *Management Science* (24:10) 1978, pp 1064-1077.

Eisenhardt, K.M. "Building theories from case study research," *Academy of Management Review* (14:4) 1989, pp 532-550.

Evans, J.S. "Strategic Flexibility for High Technology Manoeuvres: A Conceptual Framework," *Journal of Management Studies* (28:1) 1991, pp 69-89.

Gartner Group "Outsourcing Market View. What the Future Holds," Gartner Dataquest.

Hansen, M. "Knowledge networks: Explaining effective knowledge sharing in multiunit companies," in: *Organisation Science*, 2002, pp. 232-248.

Heim, G., R., and Sinha, K.K. "A Product-Process Matrix for Electronic B2C Operations: Implications for the Delivery of Customer Value," *Journal of Service Research* (3:4) 2001, pp 286-299.

Iacovou, C.L., Benbasat, I., and Dexter, A.S. "Electronic data interchange and small organizations: Adoption and impact of technology," *MIS Quarterly* (19:4) 1995, pp 465-485.

Iivari, J. "A Paradigmatic Analysis of Contemporary Schools of IS Development," *European Journal of Information Systems* (1:4) 1991, pp 249-272.

Jeyaraj, A., Rottman, J.W., and Lacity, M.C. "A review of the predictors, linkages, and biases in IT innovation adoption research," *Journal of Information Technology* (21:1) 2006, pp 1-23.

Kakabadse, A., and Kakabadse, N. "Trends in Outsourcing," *European Management Journal* (20:2) 2002, pp 189-198.

Kearns, G.S., and Lederer, A.L. "A Resource-Based View of Strategic IT Alignment: How Knowledge Sharing Creates Competitive Advantage," *Decision Sciences* (34:1) 2003, pp 1-29.

Kellog, D., and Nie, W. "A Framework for Strategic Service Management," *Journal of Operations Management* (13:4) 1995, pp 323-337.

Krcmar, H. *Informationsmanagement*, (4 ed.) Springer, Berlin, 2005.

Lacity, M.C., and Willcocks, L.P. "IT sourcing reflections - Lessons for customers and suppliers," *Wirtschaftsinformatik* (45:2) 2003, pp 115-125.

Lacity, M.C., Willcocks, L.P., and Feeny, D.F. "The Value of Selective IT Sourcing," *Sloan Management Review* (37:1) 1996, pp 13-25.

Lederer, A.L., and Mendelow, A.L. "Information resource planning: overcoming difficulties in identifying top management's objectives," *MIS Quarterly* (11:3) 1987, pp 389-399.

Lee, A.S. "A Scientific Methodology for MIS Case Studies," *MIS Quarterly* (13:1) 1989, pp 33-50.

Lee, D.M.S., Trauth, E.M., and Farwell, D. "Critical Skills and Knowledge Requirements of IS Professionals: A Joint Academic/Industry Investigation," *MIS Quarterly* (19:3) 1995, pp 313-340.

Loh, L., and Venkatraman, N. "Determinants of information technology outsourcing: A cross-sectional analysis," *Journal of Management Information Systems* (9:1) 1992, pp 7-24.

Mehta, M., and Hirschheim, R. "Strategic Alignment in Mergers and Acquisitions: Theorizing IS Integration Decision Making," *Journal of the Association for Information Systems* (8:3) 2007.

Mingers, J. "Combining IS Research Methods: Towards a Pluralist Methodology," *Information Systems Research* (12:3) 2001, pp 240-259.

Nelson, K.M., and Cooprider, J.G. "The contribution of shared knowledge to IS group performance," *MIS Quarterly* (20:4) 1996, pp 409-432.

Nelson, R., and Winter, S. *An evolutionary theory of economic change* Harvard University Press, Cambridge, MA, 1982.

Peppard, J., and Ward, J. "Mind the gap: diagnosing the relationship between the IT organization and the rest of the business," *Journal of Strategic Information Systems* (8:1) 1999, pp 29-60.

Premkumar, G., and Ramamurthy, K. "The Role of Interorganizational and Organizational Factors on the Decision Mode for Adoption of Interorganizational Systems," *Decision Sciences* (26:3) 1995, pp 303-336.

Raymond, L. "Organizational Context and Information Systems Success: A Contingency Approach," *Journal of Management Information Systems* (6:4), Spring 1990, pp 5-20.

Reich, B.H., and Benbasat, I. "Factors That Influence the Social Dimension of Alignment between Business and Information Technology Objectives," *MIS Quarterly* (24:1) 2000, pp 81-113.

Rouse, A.C., and Corbitt, B. "IT-supported business process outsourcing (BPO): The good, the bad, and the ugly," 8th Pacific-Asia Conference on Information Systems (PACIS), Shanghai, China, 2004.

Sabherwal, R., and Chan, Y.E. "Alignment between business and IS strategies: a study of prospectors, analyzers, and defenders," *Information Systems Research* (12:1) 2001a, pp 11-33.

Sabherwal, R., Hirschheim, R., and Goles, T. "The Dynamics of Alignment: Insights from a Punctuated Equilibrium Model," *Organization Science* (12:2) 2001b, pp 179-197.

Sambamurthy, V., and Zmud, R.W. "Arrangements for information technology governance: a theory of multiple contingencies," *MIS Quarterly* (23:2) 1999, pp 261-290.

Schmenner, R.W. "Service Businesses and Productivity," *Decision Sciences* (35:3) 2004, pp 333-347.

Senge, P.M. *The Leader's New Work: Building Learning Organizations* Massachusetts Institute of Technology, 1990.

Shostack, G.L. "Service Positioning through Structural Change," *Journal of Marketing* (51:1) 1987, pp 34-43.

Silvestro, R., FItzgerald, L., Johnston, R., and Voss, C. "Towards a Classification of Service Processes," *International Journal of Service Industry Management* (3:3) 1992, pp 62-75.

Snyder-Halpern, R. "Indicators of organizational readiness for clinical information technology/systems innovation: a Delphi study," *International Journal of Medical Informatics* (63:3) 2001, p 179.

Snyder, R.A., and Fields, W.L. "Measuring Hospital Readiness for Information Technology (IT) Innovation: A Multisite Study of the Organizational

Information Technology Innovation Readiness Scale," *Journal of Nursing Measurement* (14:1) 2006.

Tinnila, M., and Vepsäläinen, A.P.J. "A Model for Strategic Repositioning of Service Processes," *International Journal of Service Industry Management* (8:1) 1995, pp 37-47.

Tiwana, A., Bharadwaj, A., and Sambamurthy, V. "The antecedents of information systems development capability in firms: a knowledge integration perspective," Proceedings of the Twenty-Fourth International Conference in Information Systems, Seattle, Washington, USA, 2003, pp. 246-258.

Wagner, H.-T. *A resource-based perspective on IT business alignment and performance - Theoretical foundation and empirical evidence* ibidem, Stuttgart, Germany, 2007.

Wagner, H.-T., and Weitzel, T. "Modeling the impact of alignment routines on IT performance: an approach to making the resource based view explicit," 38th Hawaiian International Conference on Systems Sciences (HICSS-38), Waikoloa, Hawaii, 2005.

Wagner, H.-T., and Weitzel, T. "Operational IT Business Alignment as the Missing Link from IT Strategy to Firm Success," 12th Americas Conference on Information Systems (AMCIS 2006), Acapulco, Mexico, 2006.

Wahrenburg, M., König, W., Beimborn, D., Franke, J., Gellrich, T., Holzhäuser, M., Schwarze, F., and Weitzel, T. *Kreditprozess-Management* Books on Demand, Norderstedt, Germany, 2005.

Willcocks, L., Hindle, J., Feeny, D., and Lacity, M. "IT and business process outsourcing: The knowledge potential," *Information systems management* (21:3) 2004, pp 7-15.

Wüllenweber, K., Gewald, H., Franke, J., and Weitzel, T. *Business Process Outsourcing - Eine Nutzen- und Risikenanalyse in der deutschen Bankenbranche* Books on Demand, Norderstedt, Germany, 2006.

Yin, R.K. *Case study research, design and methods*, (3 ed.) Sage Publications, Beverly Hills, CA, 2002.

Zaltman, G., Duncan, R., and Holbek, J.," in: *Innovations and Organization B2 - Innovations and Organization*, John Wiley, New York, 1973.

IT Capability and Outsourcing Readiness: The Effect of Human, Technical, and Knowledge IT Resources on Outsourcing Success

Sebastian F. Martin
E-Finance Lab
Institute for Information Systems
Goethe University, Frankfurt,
Germany
smartin@wiwi.uni-frankfurt.de

Daniel Beimborn
E-Finance Lab
Institute for Information Systems
Goethe University, Frankfurt,
Germany
beimborn@wiwi.uni-frankfurt.de

Mihir A. Parikh
College of Business Administration
University of Central Florida, USA
mihir.parikh@bus.ucf.edu

Tim Weitzel
Chair of Information Systems
Bamberg University, Germany
tweitzel@wiwi.uni-frankfurt.de

Wolfgang König
E-Finance Lab
Institute for Information Systems
Goethe University, Frankfurt, Germany
koenig@wiwi.uni-frankfurt.de

Abstract

What is the impact of a client organization's IT capability on the process and the outcomes of IT outsourcing? Our insights from the qualitative investigation of a series of case studies with both outsourcing clients and vendors allow us to understand the ways in which the client's existing IT resources impact its ability to successfully prepare, implement, and conduct outsourcing relationships with external IT providers. We hereby consider three critical IT resources available to a firm: human IT resources, technical IT resources, and knowledge IT resources. We find that clients exhibiting superior IT capabilities through their

IT resources will experience fewer and lower barriers to successful IT outsourcing.

1 Introduction

Information technology (IT) outsourcing represents a major organizational transformation that requires substantial attention and knowledge in planning, transformation, and operations. Accordingly, the rich literature on outsourcing has focused on what, why, and how to outsource and disclosed, among others, the importance of contract and relationship governance. But what role does the firm's ex ante IT situation play? In this paper we look at the somewhat neglected niche of how a firm's IT resources prior to outsourcing impact its outsourcing readiness and eventually the outsourcing success. Precisely, we aim at disclosing if a firm's IT capability, consisting of its human, technical, and knowledge IT resource, constitutes a better outsourcing readiness and thereby, eventually, contributes to better achieving outsourcing goals.

It is reasonable to expect that the quality and extent of technical and business skills of the IT staff or the IT infrastructure are relevant for the success of organizational transformation in general and outsourcing in particular. Broadbent et al. (1999) show that a basic level of IT infrastructure capabilities is required for successful business process redesign and that firms which exhibit higher levels of IT infrastructure capabilities can implement more extensive changes within shorter time frames. Moreover, in an empirical investigation Bharadwaj (2000) find a positive relationship between superior human and technical IT capabilities and firm performance. Regarding outsourcing, Ross and Westerman (2004, p.5) note that "the firms' ability to generate value from outsourcing depends on the maturity of their IT architectures". Ranganathan and Balaji (2007) identify ten capabilities critical for the success of offshore outsourcing projects.

Hence, some authors have pointed out the importance of clients being properly prepared before engaging into inter-organizational cooperation (e.g., Barthélemy 2001; Ranganathan and Balaji 2007). However, these references are largely anecdotal and lack in-depth analyses, and prior empirical studies have so far failed to systematically consider the effect of client's IT resources and resulting capabilities on outsourcing success. One notable exception are Han et al. (2008) who analyze, among other factors, the effect of client's "technical and managerial IT capability" on relationship formation processes between clients and providers, which are antecedents of outsourcing success. Surprisingly, given the insights from the literature on the importance of human and technical IT resources as enablers for successful organizational transformation, their study did not, though, find statistical evidence for a significant impact of client's IT capability on these antecedents of outsourcing success.

In this paper, our aim is hence to investigate the ways in which an organization's existing IT resources may impact the preparation, implementation, and maintenance of outsourcing relationships. We consider three critical IT resources available to a firm (Bharadwaj 2000): human IT resources; technical IT resources; and knowledge IT resources. Human IT resources refer to the technical and managerial competence of IT personnel in the client firm. Technical IT resources refer to the state of the technological infrastructure and information systems in the client firm. Knowledge IT resources refer to the degree of externalization of firm-specific IT knowledge in form of documentations. Drawing on prior findings from the literature, our starting premise is that firms exhibiting superior IT capabilities through their IT resources will experience fewer and lower barriers to successful IT outsourcing. The results of our qualitative investigation of a series of case studies with both, outsourcing clients and vendors, confirm this premise and allow us to understand the ways in which the client's IT resources impact its ability to successfully prepare, implement, and conduct outsourcing relationships with IT vendors. Our insights complement the findings of (2008) and enrich the body of the outsourcing literature by further shifting the research focus on the client's preparedness for outsourcing, which up to now has only been a minor factor of research activities. We find that explaining outsourcing success or failure may not only root in factors like incomplete or faulty outsourcing contracts, in the selection of inadequate providers or bad relationship management, but may also result from missing outsourcing readiness on the client side.

2 Research Model

2.1 IT Outsourcing

The primary purpose of this study is to explain whether and how a client firm's IT resources contribute to the success (or failure) of an outsourcing venture. Generically, outsourcing can be defined as the process or the result of shifting a firm's activity from inside to outside the firm's boundaries (Dibbern 2004; Lei and Hitt 1995). IT outsourcing, in particular, is defined as the delegation of IT operations to an external service provider (Loh and Venkatraman 1992).

During the last 15 years, a mature research strand on IT outsourcing has appeared, answering the questions on why and what to outsource, on how to design the contract and how to manage the ongoing relationship, and on what the actual outcomes resulting from this fundamental organizational change are (Dibbern et al. 2004). Within this strand, scholars have developed several frameworks for describing outsourcing phenomena along various dimensions, such as outsourcing degree (selective vs. total outsourcing) (Lacity et al. 1996), type of outsourcing object (from ICT infrastructure to business process outsourcing), and governance mode (Peng and Wenhua 2004).

While Lacity et al. (1996) have emphasized the value of *selective* outsourcing of particular pieces of IT activities, this form of outsourcing leads to high interdependencies and potential points of failure between the outsourced activities and those left in the firm. The question that consequently emerges is:

How does a firm's IT infrastructure have to be designed in order to guarantee successful outsourcing of particular pieces (such as single applications) or activities (such as application development or operations)? In the sections below, we develop propositions on how several dimensions of IT infrastructure, such as modularity and degree of standardization, but also skills of the IT personnel (i.e., the "human IT infrastructure" of the firm (Byrd and Turner 2001b)), are responsible for achieving outsourcing success.

We define outsourcing success as reaching the anticipated outsourcing goals and establishing the outsourcing relationship with an external service provider without the occurrence of major delays or non-anticipated extra costs. This definition makes allowance for the fact that firms contemplating outsourcing "want to know – before the formal decision to outsource – where the money will be going and how much they can expect to spend. And after the outsourcing effort is over, they want to see the effect of these costs" (Barthélemy 2001, p. 60-61).

Outsourcing an activity happens in several phases which all have to be successfully accomplished in order to eventually achieve outsourcing success (Ilie and Parikh 2004). For the purpose of our analysis, it is reasonable to distinguish between preparation, transition, and the ongoing relationship. Preparation represents Decision to Outsource, Vendor Selection and Outsourcing Contract phases containing a strategic analysis of outsourcing options (what, why, to whom), selecting an adequate provider, closing the contract and going through a due diligence. Transition represents the implementation phase in which the outsourcing object is transferred to the vendor, often not only covering the migration of software and/or hardware assets, but also people. Relationship represents the Operations/Relationship phase in which the operational relationship between vendor and client is set up and managed.

2.2 Role of IT Resources and Capabilities for Outsourcing Success

As mentioned in the introduction, literature has acknowledged so far that a firm's technical and human IT resources play an important role as a means for achieving competitive advantage (Davenport and Linder 1994; Ross et al. 1996), as enablers for successful organizational transformation (Broadbent et al. 1999), and as drivers for firm performance (Bharadwaj 2000).

When moving from internal provisioning of IT services to outsourcing, Ross and Westerman (Ross and Westerman 2004) note that clients will be confronted with technological and organizational change challenges because outsourcing "may involve moving applications to a new environment or linking outsourced and internal applications" and "employees may, purposely or through insufficient understanding, undermine potential benefits by failing to adapt to new processes, culture, technology, or employee arrangements" (Ross and Westerman 2004, p.7). Therefore, firms need to be able to leverage their existing IT resources in order to cope with these challenges. In the following, we will discuss the ways in which clients' internal IT resources – namely, the human IT resources, the technical IT resources, and the knowledge IT resources (Bharadwaj 2000) – may affect their ability to generate value from outsourcing.

2.2.1 Human IT Resources

Following Han et al. (2008) we expect that client firms require some level of IT competence in order to effectively prepare, implement, and maintain an outsourcing relationship. Even though they did not find statistical evidence for this relation, the assumption is backed by other prior findings which indicate that the technical and managerial competence of IT professionals on the client side as well as their business competence may represent powerful impact factors for successful outsourcing. For example, Feeny and Willcocks (1998) advocate that firms should retain within their own organization nine core IT-related capabilities which relate to business and IT vision, design of IT architecture, and delivery of IS services. Each of these capabilities ultimately pertains to skills and abilities of human IT resources which, in the vision of Feeny and Willcocks, firms should keep hold of. In a later paper, Willcocks et al. (2004) describe the potential risks arising from the loss of knowledge and skills through outsourcing, stating that the loss of knowledge and information may become traumatic for the client.

The insight that, besides IT competence, IT professionals also needed *business* competence to successfully accomplish their tasks has long been pointed out in prior literature. For example, Basselier and Benbasat (2004, p.674) note that "the relationship-building ability of IT professionals has become a core capability of organizations" while Todd et al. (1995, pp.1-2) suggest that "a successful IS professional blends technical knowledge with a sound understanding of the business and interpersonal skills". This kind of competence, which does not directly pertain to one's original competencies, has been called "boundary skills" by Byrd and Turner, who highlight "the importance of IT personnel having skills and knowledge to assume roles outside their area of training or original competencies" (2001b, p.44). These boundary skills may pertain to areas like project management but also to people management and vendor management. Bassellier and Benbasat (2004) propose a taxonomy of business competence of IT professionals which comprises two dimensions: organization-specific competence and interpersonal and management competence. They state that IT professionals needed both, a thorough understanding of their organization's business model and structure as well as interpersonal, communication, and leadership skills. Based on these findings and assertions, we propose that

P1: Technical and IT management competence of the client firm's IT staff positively affects outsourcing success.

P2: Business competence of the client firm's IT staff positively affects outsourcing success.

2.2.2 Technical IT Resources

IT technical resources have multiple dimensions. Flexibility of and the degree of standardization in technical infrastructure is particularly important in an outsourcing context. Duncan (1995, p.51) notes that "flexibility of infrastructure includes the ability to support a variety of unplanned outsourcing solutions to IT problems". Flexibility of technical IT infrastructure has been discussed by several authors to be a function of two distinct factors: its *modularity* and its ability to support *integration* (Byrd and Turner 2001b; Chung et al. 2005). Modularity, which "has to do with isolating and standardizing as many business and systems processes as possible" (Duncan 1995, p.48) simplifies the extraction of IT systems from their current environment by limiting the changes that need to be performed to the system itself as well as to adjacent systems (Beimborn et al. 2008), and by reducing complexity and specificity (Lacity et al. 1996). As for the second factor, Chung et al. note that the ability of infrastructure to support integration helps spanning organizational boundaries and enables seamless and effective flows of information and work between organizations (Chung et al. 2003). Moreover, Rottmann and Lacity (2006) underline the importance of this ability, stating that clients often underestimate the difficulties of integrating providers into the structures and workflows of their companies. We thus propose that

P3: A flexible (i.e., modular and integrative) client IT infrastructure positively impacts outsourcing success.

With regard to systems standardization, Duncan notes that the organizational decision to adopt a certain technological standard may restrict the variety of available outsourcing choices for client firms (Duncan 1995). However, if mainstream standards are employed, standardization may also have the reverse effect, *increasing* the firm's array of choices regarding possible outsourcing providers and facilitating systems integration (Lacity et al. 1995). This is because providers' business models are often based on the achievement of economies of scale, which occur by bundling several client systems on a common – standardized – platform. Thus, many providers specialize in offering IT services for a specific mainstream standard like SAP. Moreover, Ross and Westerman note that "firms unaccustomed to standardization [...] experience resistance to vendor initiatives, and thus run the risk of missing out on their potential benefits" (Ross and Westerman 2004, p.13). Therefore, we propose that

P4: Standardization of client's technical IT infrastructure positively impacts outsourcing success.

2.2.3 Knowledge IT Resources

Prior literature has largely recognized the importance of intangibles like organizational knowledge (Bharadwaj 2000). Indeed, the core of the arguments made above is that it is all about knowledge that resides in either the IT staff (human IT resource) or has manifested as IT architecture (technical IT resource). But this leaves open codified knowledge as an important other knowledge source. We believe that the availability of explicit knowledge in form of documentation (e.g., systems and process documentation, operating figures, etc.) plays an important role in an outsourcing context. When implementing an outsourcing relationship, the provider needs to acquire a detailed understanding of the client's systems (Dibbern et al. 2008) and processes. Thus, there is a need for intense knowledge transfer between client and provider, which is even greater if proprietary systems, as opposed to standardized systems, are being outsourced. (Weitzel 2006) empirically shows that "documentation ... is a necessary yet often neglected prerequisite for efficiency improvements" and that analyses based on such documentation positively impact a firm's likelihood to consider outsourcing a valid option. Using a relationship perspective, the availability of explicit knowledge in form of detailed documentation allows for more effective knowledge transfer between client and provider (Lee 2001). Using a transaction cost perspective (Wüllenweber et al. 2008) empirically show that process documentation positively impacts outsourcing success because of increased transparency. Martin et al. (2008) found that documentation, as a source of explicit knowledge for the outsourcing provider, moderates the impact of IT provider's tacit knowledge on its flexibility such that high-quality documentation made the provider's tacit knowledge on flexibility less of a limiting factor (Martin et al. 2008). For client organizations, this means that the availability of good documentation mitigates, to some degree, the necessity to find a provider that is highly acquainted with the client's system particularities, because the provider can draw on existing documentation as a source of information. We thus propose that

P5: The availability of thorough documentation positively impacts outsourcing success.

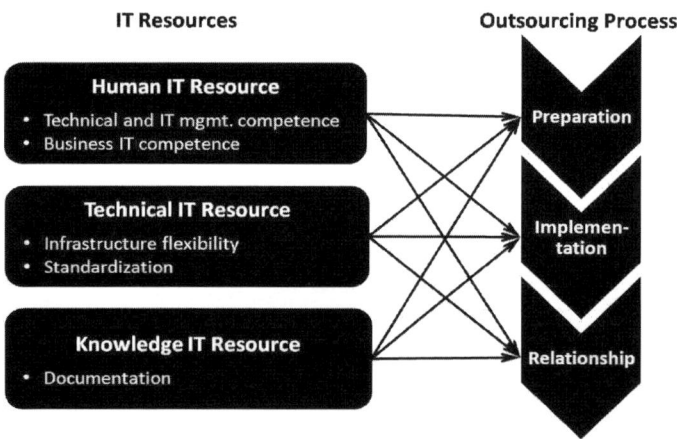

Figure 1: Research Model

Figure 1 summarizes the proposed impact of client's infrastructure on the successful preparation, implementation, and maintenance of outsourcing relationships. Through case studies, we seek to understand and document the mechanisms through which these characteristics impact outsourcing success.

3 Methodology

3.1 Research Design

Since we have built our research model based on prior literature, the research methodology chosen for this study follows the positivist paradigm. Our research question is a typical *"how"*-question in the nomenclature of Yin (2003) (i.e., *how client's IT resources affect the successful preparation, implementation, and maintenance of IT outsourcing*). According to Yin (2003), effectively pursuing this kind of question requires a qualitative approach, which, given the fact that we are analyzing previously hypothesized links, is explanatory in nature. We chose a two-step approach to pursue our research question. In the first stage, we conducted a case study with a large IT outsourcing provider, aiming to understand the different associations between the preparedness of client's IT resources and the successful preparation, implementation and maintenance of IT outsourcing relationships. In the second stage, we performed two case studies with client firms from the financial industry, aiming to validate the findings from the first stage.

3.2 Site Selection

3.2.1 Stage 1: Provider Case

In the first stage of our qualitative study, we carried out multiple interviews with eight senior managers from a large IT services provider. This firm employs about 2,000 people in Germany and has specialized in providing IT application management and consulting services to a wide range of customers from different industries, with a core focus on the financial industry. The interviewed managers featured an average of 12 years of experience in the outsourcing field and have conducted an average of 16 outsourcing projects along their career. We carried out several rounds of face to face discussions with each of the eight managers, complemented by E-mail exchange and clarifying phone conversations when needed.

We chose to carry out this first set of interviews with managers from the provider side because asking provider managers with extensive experience in the outsourcing domain would allow us to collect aggregated insights from multiple outsourcing projects. Moreover, the particular firm at which the interviewed managers are employed is a large and established outsourcing provider for application management with a wide portfolio of clients of different sizes and from different branches (financial services, automotive, etc). This way, we were in the best position to produce findings which were likely to be valid across an array of industries and firm sizes.

3.2.2 Stage 2: Client Cases

The aim of the second stage was to validate the findings from the first stage through two representative client case studies. From the two cases, the first case was a successful outsourcing project, while the second case represents a failed outsourcing project, which had to be aborted prematurely. The two cases are described in more detail below.

Client Alpha

The first client case is a German retail bank with about 6,000 employees and about 1.5 million retail customers. In 2004, management decided to outsource a back office application concerned with the processing of returned mail. Our interview partner here was the project manager who initiated and carried out the outsourcing project. For a better understanding of the findings, in the following we briefly describe the business process supported by the outsourced application. Parts of this business process were outsourced together with the supporting application.

From the total amount of letters sent by the bank to its customers, a certain amount is undeliverable and is being returned to the sender because the addressee cannot be reached. While much of this returned mail is being dumped, there is however legally binding correspondence that makes it necessary for the bank to undertake further investigations to find out the addressee's new location. For this, the bank needs to make an inquiry at the so-called citizen registration office – an institution that basically exists in every German city. The office then either sends back the new address of that person – in which case the bank simply updates its records and redirects the mail – or returns an answer that makes it necessary for the bank to send a so-called extended inquiry to either that or another registration office. For example, the addressee may be deceased, in which case the bank may need to ask for the decease date and death certificate. Or an answer like "moved to Berlin" – i.e., without a concrete address – comes back, in which case the bank needs to approach the citizen registration office in Berlin to locate that person. On average, the bank needs to make about 3,000 such "extended inquiries", as they are called, per month. While most registration offices – the bank needs to deal with about 200 different offices throughout the country – have an automated interface for this kind of inquiries, these interfaces are not standardized so that for each registration office the inquiry needs to be sent in a particular format. The bank had an application in place that automated some of the steps of the extended inquiry process. However, managers felt they could cut costs by outsourcing the management and further development of the application together with parts of the extended inquiry process to a specialized service provider.

Client Beta

The second client case (Client Beta) is a 100% subsidiary of a large German Bank, concerned with IT service provision for its parent company, with about 1,500 employees. In 2005, the management board decided to outsource the operations and maintenance of its telecommunications infrastructure – i.e. operations and maintenance of the telecommunications backbone and of the office telecommunications equipment (terminals and servers). Our interview partner here was the head of the telecommunications department, who was involved in the outsourcing project from the beginning.

After the outsourcing decision was made by the top management, the firm immediately started negotiations with a provider with whom they had worked together before in other areas. It was the only provider with whom they started negotiations. After two years of project duration, the management board "pulled the emergency break", aborting the project even before the contract with the provider was signed and dropping any further outsourcing plans for that IT function. A three-hour interview with the leader of the telecommunications department gave us good insights about the substantial contribution of the unpreparedness of the firm's IT resources to the failure of the project.

3.3 Data Collection and Data Analysis

Throughout the two stages of the study, rigor was ensured by following the guidelines given by case study methodologists (Dubé and Paré 2003; Eisenhardt 1989; Shanks and Parr 2003; Yin 2003). Data collection was performed systematically, with a clear research focus and a pre-defined research question. Each interview was carried out by a team of two researchers, recorded on tape, and subsequently transcribed. The transcripts were aggregated into a document comprising 142,781 words on 360 pages. We used high-level, semi-structured interview guidelines to make sure that we touched all thematic areas planned for discussion, but without specifically referring to any of the IT resource characteristics introduced above. This way, we were able to minimize our influence on our interlocutor's opinion and to observe which IT characteristics emerged during the interviews and were regarded by our interview partners to be critical for outsourcing success.

Construct validity "concerns the issue of whether empirical data in multiple situations leads to the same conclusions, and is improved by multiple sources of evidence" and "having key informants review the case study report" (Shanks and Parr 2003, p. 6). To ensure construct validity, we carried out a total of ten interviews with senior managers from three different organizations – one IT service provider and two client firms. Each interview lasted between 1.5 and 3 hours. The interviews were coded independently by two researchers and the interviewed persons were then asked to review the results of the interviews and to confirm their validity, which they all did. Moreover, further evidence like process documentation and excerpts from the firm-internal websites were handed over to us by some of our interview partners.

We aimed to ensure external validity, which is concerned with the generalizability of the findings, (Shanks and Parr 2003) by choosing interlocutors with extensive experience in the outsourcing domain and explicitly asking them to share their experience from typical outsourcing cases with us (Yin 2003). Moreover, while the first stage of the study was carried out at the provider site, we chose to complement this stage with two more case studies performed at the client site in order to find evidence which would confirm or falsify our findings. Thus, we also captured a broad range of different types of outsourcing such as ICT infrastructure outsourcing, application management outsourcing, and business process outsourcing.

To ensure reliability, which "concerns the stability and consistency of the study over time" (Shanks and Parr 2003, p. 6), case study methodologists recommend the usage of a case study database and developing a clear case study protocol (Yin 2003). For data analysis, we used the software MaxQDA (version 2), which is especially designed for qualitative research, allowing for storage and coding of transcripts and offering multiple opportunities for case analysis and comparison. Finally, a case study protocol was produced by the researcher team.

Finally, we used pattern matching to ensure internal validity, comparing predication from the literature with evidence from multiple interviews in different firms (Yin 2003).

4 Findings

4.1 Effects of Human IT Resources on Outsourcing Success

Analyzing the interviews from the provider as well as the client cases, we found evidence for several ways in which technical and managerial competence as well as business competence on the client side contributes to the success of outsourcing ventures.

4.1.1 Technical and managerial IT competence

Findings from the provider side

Technical and managerial IT competence "involves technical knowledge and skills needed to develop applications" as well as the "knowledge of where and how IT is deployed effectively and profitably to meet strategic business objectives" (Han et al. 2008, p.33). Han et al. assumed that "the client firm will also require IT capabilities to be effective in monitoring a vendor's work" (2008, p.33), but failed to find empirical evidence for this assumption. Our interviews however revealed a multitude of ways by which technical and managerial IT competence may affect the outcomes of the outsourcing process.

Within the *preparation* stage of outsourcing projects, technical and technology management competence is required for assessing which parts of an IT function may be outsourced safely, for assessing the criticality of the systems subject to outsourcing for the overall business, for building contingency plans to cover cases of service failure, and for defining and negotiating the service and the output that the provider is expected to deliver (e.g., service levels and key performance indicators). In this phase, especially employees at middle-management level need to have a deep understanding of their IT landscape in order to be able to perform these tasks.

"Top management may not need it, but middle management definitely needs a detailed understanding of the IT function. Top management explores

strategies and creates the general conditions that may facilitate outsourcing. Middle management needs to have the full understanding about what exactly is "outsourceable" and what needs to be retained in-house." (Provider Manager 4)

In the *relationship phase*, thorough IT management skills are needed for monitoring the services delivered by the provider:

"IT personnel at an operational level, who will be actively managing the service provider after outsourcing, needs to have a deep understanding about the output that is being expected from the service provider. Knowledge about things like how to measure the provider's output; KPIs; what information the reports should contain – all in all: [a deep understanding of] all criteria that are required for successful service provision." (Provider Manager 4)

Even special IT management skills like ITIL certification may be required on the client side, as one of our interview partners pointed out:

"Many service providers are ITIL certified, because clients often want their IT to be managed consistently with ITIL. But, then you [the client] need to have someone in your service management team who speaks ITIL". (Provider Manager 3)

Thus, technical and managerial IT competencies seem to be necessary throughout the process of outsourcing. Their availability helps lowering barriers to proper outsourcing implementation by lowering the costs of the preparation, negotiation, and transition of the IT. If this kind of competence is not available in-house, the client needs to buy it from the market in form of consulting services.

Evidence from the client side

From our two case study participants, Client Beta had not outsourced any of its IT functions before and practically none of the involved managers had experience with outsourcing. As the negotiations went on, the service provider asked the client to specify the exact services they wanted to buy, in order to be able to calculate an offer. However, the project staff was not in the position to provide a detailed and precise description of the services they wanted to buy from the vendor. Eventually, this incapacity to specify the expected service in detail became one of the main causes for the failure of the outsourcing project.

> *"I think that one of the main reasons for the project's failure was that the provider asked us to specify what exactly we wanted them to do for us. But as a customer, when I walk into a store, I normally expect the vendor to make me an offer. Instead, the provider said: 'Tell us what exactly you need from us'." (Manager Client Beta)*

This problem could have probably been overcome if Client Beta would have hired external consultants to help out with the specification of the services they expected their partner to provide, but this never happened.

> *"Retrospectively, I realize that we should have done this, we should have hired someone from outside to point us to the right direction and help us at the negotiation table. This was an important issue." (Manager Client Beta)*

4.1.2 Business Competence

Findings from the provider side

A widely accepted framework classifies business competence into three different sub-dimensions: competencies in project management, business understanding, and leadership and interpersonal competence (Bassellier and Benbasat 2004). We found several ways by which each of the three sub-dimensions of business competence may influence the preparation, implementation, and monitoring of outsourcing relationships.

Several interview partners asserted that setting up and conducting an outsourcing project requires not just well-developed technical knowledge, but also a good sense for people and project management:

"Higher management needs to know how to motivate people [to support the outsourcing project]. They need the people-management skills to dispel the uncertainties that come along with such a project." (Provider Manager 4)

"Managers need a good portion of assertiveness because in such change processes, they will invariably encounter resistance. They need to be capable of making decisions." (Provider Manager 5)

But, people and project management skills are not only needed for the process of initially transferring the IT function and knowledge to the provider. Ongoing outsourcing relationships typically entail many smaller or larger change projects which also require thorough management and controlling.

"The service manager must be a person who knows how to manage projects. [...] He must be able to manage and he must have an understanding of both, the business process and the underlying IT. Only if he has these three issues under control may he be able to fulfill his tasks." (Provider Manager 6)

Business understanding represents another sub-dimension of the business competence of IT employees, influencing the ability of the in-house IT managers to align with the business domain. When an IT function is operated and maintained by an external provider, changes to that particular IT function may quickly become costly if change requests are not precisely and completely formulated. This matter was well-illustrated by one of our interview partners on provider side who gave us an example of how one of his clients, for whom his company was performing operations, maintenance, and enhancement services of a book-keeping system, formulates change requests:

"My experience [with this particular customer] is this: they manage to describe about 70% of the desired change at once, while the remaining 30% keep pouring along. They never manage to formulate a complete change request so they can say: 'this is it, that's what we want you to implement'. [...] If you [the client firm] perform outsourcing, you need to optimize this

process [of specifying change requests] within your own organization. You should be able to formulate a change request completely [because] 80% degree of completion generates 20% of the costs and completing the remaining 20% will generate 80% of the costs." (Provider Manager 3)

Consequently, service managers on the client side need to have a thorough business understanding because this enables them to evaluate the IT requirements of the business domain and to translate these requirements into clear and complete change requests.

"Take for example application management outsourcing. [The service manager] needs a lot of [business] process know-how. He must know the process and he must know how the process is mapped within the system." (Provider Manager 1)

"That's one of the big problems [with outsourcing]: the requirements need to be properly specified, so that later you don't have any major changes anymore." (Provider Manager 7)

Regarding the third sub-dimension of business competence – leadership and interpersonal skills – literature has repeatedly pointed out that the human resource belongs to the highest risk factors in projects involving organizational change (e.g., Armenakis et al. 1993). For some of the client's IT employees, outsourcing may go along with a change in their range of duties, job transfer, or even job loss. The incertitude about how outsourcing is going to affect one's own job needs to be addressed by management with great sensibility. For that matter, IT managers need inter-personal and communication skills that enable them to motivate their co-workers to support the project.

"I have experienced projects where the IT people leeched on to their tasks. The decision to outsource was communicated to them top-down in a very direct manner – "that's how we'll do this now" – with no regard to [the employees'] fear of job loss. This led to a subtle boycott of the project [by the

IT employees], who suddenly began to see problems and risks and motives for failure everywhere. [...] Such projects are doomed to fail, because they are not being supported by the employees. It is important to clearly communicate the aims of the project and to give the IT employees a clear perspective." (Provider Manager 4)

"You need the trust [of operative IT personnel]. This is especially delicate when personnel transfer [from the outsourcer to the service provider] is planned; but even without personnel transfer you need [the IT employee's] trust. He doesn't know what's going to become of him. He will offer resistance [against outsourcing]. He will try to prove that this outsourcing deal won't work." (Provider Manager 5)

Interpersonal skills are also needed by the service management – i.e., the in-house IT personnel who will be managing the provider. IT employees whose responsibilities change from technology-oriented to management-oriented tasks may simply lack the necessary boundary skills to cope with their new responsibilities. Our interview partners pointed out that often their clients did not pay enough attention to this matter, which may become critical if not properly addressed. Especially former IT technicians who after outsourcing become service managers need to have or be able to acquire the necessary interpersonal and management skills to manage the vendor:

"I have often seen this in client firms: the internal IT guys they used to employ were typical geeks – guys who really enjoyed IT. And while today they administrate databases, tomorrow they need to manage other people who administer the same databases. This is a highly explosive matter, one that is being underestimated by many firms. Not every database administrator may become a good service manager, one that knows how to manage the service provider. [...]" (Provider Manager 4)

Evidence from the client side

Again, the case of Client Beta is illustrative for how missing interpersonal and communication competence of the IT management led to outsourcing failure. While pursuing the outsourcing project, management tried not to create panic among the employees by not communicating the intention to outsource, with dramatic effects:

> *"There was a communication problem for which we, the executives, were clearly responsible. [...] You cannot keep such an outsourcing project secret. This is what happens: soon, 'radio hallway' starts broadcasting. People talk about it. 'Did you hear anything?' 'Yeah, but I'm not allowed to tell.' This is exactly the kind of thing that paralyzes an organization. During this time [the course of the outsourcing preparation] we achieved very little progress, simply because people were unmotivated. [...] This is the worst thing that can happen to an organization."* (Manager Client Beta)

The following table summarizes our findings regarding the different aspects of IT personnel competence and the ways by which these aspects may affect outsourcing success.

Dimension		Competencies	Impact on outsourcing		
			Preparation phase	Transition phase	Ongoing relationship
Human IT Resource	Technical and managerial competence (Han et al. 2008)	Technical		Identify hyphenation points for extracting the systems that are to be outsourced from their current technological environment	
				Perform required changes to adjacent systems which are kept in-house	
		Technology management	Formulate SLAs and KPIs; Assess criticality of systems for the overall business; Elaborate contingency plans		Monitor the output provided by the outsourcing partner
	Business competence (Bassellier and Benbasat 2004; Byrd and Turner 2001a)	Project management	Plan and manage costs, people, time, and quality criteria of outsourcing projects.		
		Leadership and interpersonal	Motivate personnel to accept and support outsourcing; disclose personal perspectives for affected employees		
		Business function	Align with business domain		
					Formulate and prioritize changes

Table 1: How the Human IT Resource affects outsourcing success

4.2 Effects of Technical IT Resources on Outsourcing Success

4.2.1 IT Infrastructure Flexibility

Findings from the provider side

Infrastructure flexibility has been largely discussed to be a necessary factor for the competitiveness of organizations. Flexible IT infrastructures allow organizations to quickly adapt their technological components in order to support new business needs. IT flexibility has been described in prior literature to be a function of two different factors which we will discuss separately in the following sections.

The first factor is the infrastructural ability to support secure and easy integration of different technological components as a means for enhanced information sharing and processing. Keen describes integration ability in terms of "reach and range" of the IT platform (Keen 1993), while other authors refer to this ability as the degree of compatibility and connectivity of the IT components (Byrd and Turner 2001b; Chung et al. 2005).

The importance of this factor for successful ITO implementation cannot be overemphasized. Seamless integration makes it possible for the provider to offer IT services as if the IT were operated in-house:

"Take for example our client [car manufacturer]. We provide application management for them, but the infrastructure is located at the client side. It is imperative that we have an integrated solution in place. It doesn't help if we are running our own ticketing system that it is not interconnected with the client's applications. We need a bridge to our client's systems that insures a clean communication with our project partners." (Provider Manager 5)

Of course, the integration with external partners should not put at risk the security and privacy of firm-internal data. The client's IT infrastructure must allow him to protect his data from unauthorized access through the provider, who otherwise might gain access to confidential information, as well as through third parties, who may intercept the inter-organizational communication flow. Security aspects regarding the integration with external partners were pointed out by six of our eight interview partners on provider side to be among the most sensible issues when performing outsourcing. Lacking infrastructural security may lead to serious drawbacks and delays in the project if not properly considered in the initial outsourcing phases:

"You need an infrastructure that supports data encryption for remote access. This is imperative for outsourcing. You might not need remote access at all, but if you or the provider need to access a system remotely, then the information flow may be recorded by others if it's not encrypted." (Provider Manager 7)

"Privacy is a very important aspect. If, for example, you outsource a system for travelling costs management, then you must ensure that the service

> *provider will not be able to access the databases where you keep your production records."* (Provider Manager 7)

> *"Are all necessary security measures, firewalls, etc. implemented? These aspects are a basic prerequisite [for outsourcing]. If you [the client] don't have this under control, it's a no go."* (Provider Manager 5)

Missing integration ability also poses the risk of management not implementing necessary integrated solutions due to high costs of systems development and adaptation. Our interview partners pointed us to the often-neglected necessity of implementing systems for the seamless transfer of information about fault states of the IT. How can, for example, any occurring incidents be communicated by the client's users to the service provider's IT specialists? Is there an incidence communication system in place or do users need to describe the failure by phone or via email? Conversely, does the infrastructure in place support the transfer of knowledge from the provider to the outsourcer during the course of the relationship?

> *"How do users from the business department articulate any occurring incidents and send them over to help desk? Is there an integrated ticketing system in place? You need an infrastructure [for failure management]. If you don't have this, things get complicated... it's unprofessional. You definitely need to implement one."* (Provider Manager 8)

> *"It's helpful to have a ticketing system that guides the user into describing the problem. It's helpful if you have checklists and input masks, in which the user can insert his computer ID, phone number, etc. [Problem solving] will never work if you don't have a ticketing system in place and everything is provided freely via email."* (Provider Manager 3)

The second factor that defines IT flexibility is the "ability to add, modify, and remove any software, hardware, or data components of the infrastructure with ease and with no major overall effect" (Byrd and Turner 2000, p.171), which has been termed "modularity" by several authors. Without modularity, extracting deeply integrated systems from their current environment may have unforeseeable impacts on adjacent systems. Modular systems allow for clear "cuts" between the parts that are to be outsourced and the parts of the system that remain in-house, thus helping to lower the barriers to IT outsourcing implementation, while missing modularity may cause unforeseen and costly implications. As Schilling notes, "the components of almost all systems are ultimately separable, although much may be lost in their separation" (Schilling 2000, p.215). One of our interview partners recalled an example of missing modularity from one of the outsourcing projects he was involved with, pointing out that the partners had to later on call for external consultants to help them fix the negative consequences of imprecisely defined and separated modules:

"[When outsourcing], the cuts had been set imprecisely... they had cut through life arteries. They should have thought more carefully about how [the system] could be partitioned." (Provider Manager 5)

Evidence from the client side

The integration issue played a special role in the case of Client Alpha. First, the inability of the firm to build up and maintain seamless communication channels with each of the registration offices was the primary reason for outsourcing. This is why they decided to outsource this task to a specialized service provider. However, their infrastructure allowed for seamless integration with the service provider who from there on acted as a communication hub between Client Alpha and the different registration offices. Second, the particular service provider was chosen because it was the only one available on the market to offer an integrated solution for data transfer.

"With some firms which offer this service, you need to access a portal and enter the data manually. But we wanted more than that. We wanted a widely

automated solution, one that could be integrated with our systems. This was exactly the value added this supplier could offer". (Manager Client Alpha)

In the case of Client Beta, the issue of secure integration played a decisive role. One of the reasons for the abortion of the outsourcing project was that absolute data security could not be ensured when interconnecting with the service provider:

"There's nothing worse for a bank than a security leak that's being made public. It's already bad enough that they talk so much about this topic in the media these days – be it phishing or other things you hear about on TV. And we said: we can't afford this. One mistake here could all at once undo all the benefits that we might get from outsourcing." (Manager Client Beta)

4.2.2 Standardization

Findings from the provider side

Standardization was indicated by our interview partners to be a huge facilitator for successful outsourcing. The main idea here is that standardized systems and applications are usually easier to outsource for a number of reasons. First, the variety of service offerings for standardized applications is higher and a suitable provider is more likely to be found since for the providers the risks of insourcing a standard application are lower because of the widespread availability of deep knowledge about that application, which for example makes trouble-shooting easier. Moreover, a wide array of available providers reduces the threat of strategic dependence (lock-in).

"You're much better off if you have standard software in place. If you want to outsource custom software it'll be much more complicated. For example, you don't have the same range of choices regarding providers. You'll find plenty of firms who offer SAP outsourcing services today, because running SAP for different businesses is only a matter of different shades, it's not something fundamentally different. But [for custom software], you will first need to find

a suitable provider who will be willing to offer this service [...]. That's because for the provider, the risks are much higher. [With proprietary systems,] he may be the last one in the chain, the one who has to solve the problem, should any failures occur. With standard software like SAP, he can always go to SAP and ask for help with any special problems." (Provider Manager 7)

Second, there is less need for extensive knowledge transfer related to the systems subject to outsourcing when these systems represent an industry standard. On the other hand, thorough documentation of systems alleviates to some degree the disadvantages that arise from missing standardization:

"If you have standardized, commercial software in your company – say for example SAP –, then you already have a good starting position. At least part of the basic infrastructure may then be outsourced without problems because you have standardized, well-known specifications made by the software producer. If, instead, it's a proprietary application you want to outsource, then [success] very much depends on how well this software is documented." (Provider Manager 4)

"Handing-over a proprietary application may turn into a herculean effort." (Provider Manager 7)

Third, the size of the application in terms of service costs is less of an issue because the provider may realize synergies by bundling applications from different clients.

"How big is the package you want to outsource? If it's a small package, let's say one that needs only one person to be run by, you might have trouble finding a service provider, especially if it is a proprietary application. [...] In your own firm, if the guy who runs the application is on vacation, things may just have to wait until he's back. But the service provider usually needs to ensure 24/7 service provision. So at least two persons will need to get

accustomed with that application on provider side... Fallback issues may therefore become very costly if the application is too small..." (Provider Manager 2)

"You might, for example, want to outsource your SAP system. An IT outsourcing provider may already manage 150 SAP systems or more. This gives him a lot of synergetic potential which translates into cost benefits." (Provider Manager 4)

Evidence from the client side

In the case of Client Alpha, the application subject to outsourcing was proprietary software. This may appear to be in contradiction with the evidence from the provider interviews, since the outsourcing project of Client Alpha proved very successful. But in this particular case, the application was initially developed by the same provider to which the bank now decided to outsource the application together with the supported business process. Consequently, in this special case the provider already knows the system better than the client does. If it were not for this particular provider, Client Alpha would have had great difficulties in finding another service provider.

The following table summarizes our findings regarding the different aspects of technical IT infrastructure and the ways in which these aspects may affect successful outsourcing.

Dimension		Aspect	Impact on outsourcing		
			Preparation phase	Transition phase	Ongoing relationship
Technical IT Resource	Flexibility (Byrd and Turner 2000; Byrd and Turner 2001b)	Integration	Facilitate the interconnection of the partner's systems with the own systems; enable seamless information transfer and processing between the partners		
		Modularity	Eases the identification of hyphenation points and the extraction of the systems that are subject to outsourcing from their current environment		
	Standardization (Wüllenweber et al. 2008; Wüllenweber and Weitzel 2007)		Acts as an enabler for flexibility; allows for easier interconnection between partners	Reduces the need for extensive knowledge transfer between client and provider	
			Allows for a wider array of choices among specialized providers		

Table 2: How the Technical IT Resource affects outsourcing success

4.3 Effects of Knowledge IT Resources on Outsourcing Success

Findings from the provider side

We found strong support for the influence of documentation as a source of formalized explicit knowledge (Nonaka 1994) on successful outsourcing. Most of our eight interview partners on provider side repeatedly pointed out documentation to be a required prerequisite for proper outsourcing preparation as well as for know-how transfer within the implementation and relationship phases, especially if proprietary or unique systems and applications are outsourced.

In the *preparation phase* of an outsourcing deal, good documentation helps IT technicians to identify potential hyphenation points, where the IT function may be split between client and provider, to extract the systems from their current technological environment and to make the necessary changes to adjacent systems. Moreover, systems documentation like detailed logs about the system activity (e.g., peak times and access control) may provide the basis for the formulation of service level agreements and key performance indicators.

"At least the part [of the system] which you want to outsource should be neatly described. The interfaces and everything. This is imperative." (Provider Manager 1)

"Important for outsourcing is that you have statistics, analyses from the run phase. You need to know details about the operation time: how many tickets have accrued? Are there any peak times when errors tend to appear? Some applications become especially vulnerable in certain months, for example around year-end closing. The more information I can hand over to the service provider, the more precise the agreement with him can become. If I cannot tell him anything, he won't be able to tell me a reliable price [for his service]." (Provider Manager 3)

Within the *implementation phase*, existing documentation forms the basis for effective knowledge transfer, improving the provider's ability and chances to quickly become acquainted with the client's systems and processes.

"It is very important that the operations be well-documented [because] you need a thorough basis for the transition phase. Otherwise you'll need to have your experts produce a basic documentation during the transition phase and hand it over [to the service provider] as a basis for the cooperation." (Provider Manager 7)

During the *relationship phase*, good documentation helps the providers to react to their clients' change requests with speed and accuracy (Martin et al. 2008). The less documentation exists about the system, the more costly it becomes if the provider has to perform any specific changes because, without a source of explicit knowledge, he needs to draw on the client's tacit knowledge or has to create own knowledge about that system. Both alternatives are of course costly and time consuming.

"We once had to change an application for a bank from Luxemburg – they didn't have the source code anymore. There really was only the running application. But what exactly did this application do? We had to record the data traffic and work our way up from the data traffic to the functionality in order to restore the software." (Provider Manager 3)

As with missing standardization, good documentation also alleviates to some degree the disadvantages stemming from missing flexibility of the IT infrastructure. The less modular and more interweaved a system is to its surrounding environment, the more difficult it becomes to extract that system from its technological environment without being able to draw on good documentation. This complementary relationship was constantly highlighted by our interview partners and is illustrated by the following quotation:

> "The aspect of clear interfaces and interconnectedness is important. Heavily interconnected applications with no clear partitions are much harder to outsource than applications with well-defined boundaries. It's a matter of complexity, and there is also the important aspect of privacy and security. [...] You need good documentation. The interfaces must be all well-described." (Provider Manager 6)

Evidence from the client side

At Client Alpha, a great deal of attention was given to documenting the knowledge related to the firm's IT and business processes which existed in the organization. This fact was considered to be one of the main reasons for outsourcing success. The bank had focused immensely in the last years on documenting all its regular processes, as a result of major restructuration that had to be performed in order to save the bank from bankruptcy. The bank even had a detailed "how to" guide for outsourcing projects, which described in great detail who had to be informed, which steps had to be performed, etc.

> "[A few years ago], we were short to closure. We had quite a big problem with real-estate credits. [...] We were saved [but] the European Commission imposed exact conditions about which business segments we had to give up and which ones we were allowed to keep. During the restructuring phase, we were forced to build a very, very detailed process catalogue. For each of our today's regular activities we have specification sheets where the resources

and costs of every single process step are described correct to a dot." (Manager Client Alpha)

"An important factor of success for us was that we knew exactly what we wanted to outsource. [...] Almost every single handgrip was documented in great detail." (Manager Client Alpha)

"We use ARIS1 to describe all our business processes. And for processes like the one that has been partially outsourced, we have detailed figures for every step: time spent per number of items, bound capacities, etc. [...] Process documentation is always holistic in our house. The process chain starts in the front-end at the customer and goes all the way to back-office. [...] And so does the documentation. Each process is documented starting with the product and documentation goes throughout every involved department." (Manager Client Alpha)

By contrast, missing documentation played an important role in the failure of Client Beta's outsourcing project. Employees were not willing and were not constrained to document their work in great detail. This is why much of Client Beta's documentation was too superficial to be of any use for outsourcing preparation.

"Let's say we perform a change to our voice platform. This change is being recorded, but the protocol just briefly summarizes: 'change done' or 'request has been carried-out'. But it doesn't say 'we had to apply this patch to the operating system on the server to fulfill the request'. [...] We never reached this level of granularity. [...] As a consequence, you can only outsource to someone who already deploys this kind of system and has the necessary background knowledge." (Manager Client Beta)

---

[1] *ARIS is a business process management approach used by firms to document their processes and organizations. For example, it is implemented as primary modeling approach in SAP software.*

"In my personal opinion, we would have never been able to accurately describe the parts we wanted to outsource. Every organization consists of people. And people fear for their working places. And this is what happens: they do not document their knowledge; they keep it in their heads. Especially in the IT, we have many 'head monopolies'. People are not willing to document their work [...]. They say: 'if I document my work in every detail, then they'll be able to outsource my job to China or India'." (Manager Client Beta)

The following table summarizes our findings concerning the ways by which documentation may affect the preparation, the implementation, as well as the ongoing relationship between client firm and IT provider.

	Impact on outsourcing		
	Preparation phase	Transition phase	Ongoing relationship
Knowledge IT Resource	Helps to identify necessary changes to adjacent systems and business processes;	Helps to improve knowledge transfer between client and provider by providing a source of explicit knowledge. Alleviates to some degree the disadvantages stemming from missing standardization and modularity.	Improves provider flexibility and lowers the costs of change implementations.
	Provides information basis for contract specification and formulation of SLAs and KPIs		

Table 3: How the Knowledge IT Resource affects outsourcing success

As a summary, Table 4 gives an overview on the number of quotations from provider side pertaining to the particular aspects of each dimension. Moreover, the right columns show whether the dimension played a role for outsourcing success or failure, respectively, in the investigated client cases.

Resource	Dimension	Sub-Dimension	Total no. of quotations in provider interviews	Found relevance for project success Client Alpha?	Found relevance for project failure Client Beta?
Human IT resources	Technical and managerial competence	Technical	10	No	No
		Technology management	17	No	Yes
	Business competence	Project management	4	No	Yes
		Leadership and interpersonal	22	No	Yes
		Business function	9	No	No
Technical IT resources	Flexibility	Integration	30	Yes	Yes
		Modularity	9	No	No
	Standardization		13	Yes	No
Knowledge IT resources			50	Yes	Yes

Table 4: Quantitative overview of quotations

5 Discussion and Conclusion

Our analysis reveals an important effect of human, technical and knowledge IT resources on the eventual success or failure of outsourcing. An in-depth investigation of vendor and client side cases showed several ways by which each of these elements can influence the process of outsourcing and the subsequent relationship between client and IT provider.

To complement the case analysis so far, comparing the number of references to the different aspects of each element suggests that technology management competencies and soft skills (leadership and interpersonal) are the most decisive facets of the Human IT resource. From a technical perspective, the ability of the IT infrastructure to support easy and secure integration with internal and external systems seems to be more important than modularity and standardization. This corresponds with the conclusions of Byrd and Turner (2001b) who find that integration, as a dimension of IT infrastructure flexibility, is more important for competitive advantage than modularity. However, one has to bear in mind that modularity is a rather new concept which is not a common feature of the infrastructures of today's organizations. Since our interlocutors shared with us their experience from their daily business, this may be a reason why modularity has not received more emphasis during the discussions. With the possible increased adoption of service-oriented architectures by firms, managers may learn to appreciate the advantages of modularity.

Because of the particularities of the client side cases, some of the findings were not relevant in the particular context and we could thus not match all findings from the provider case with the client cases. Besides missing client side evidence for the effect of modularity, which we ascribe to the above-discussed reasons, we could not validate the effect of technical skills and of IT managers' business function competence on outsourcing success. With regard to technical skills, in the case of Client Alpha the application subject to outsourcing was already known in detail by the service provider, since it was this particular service provider who also developed that system for Client Alpha a while ago. In the case of Client Beta, the project was still in an early phase when it was abandoned, and technical skills, which would have especially been required in the transition phase, did not get to play a role. With regard to IT managers' business function competence, our findings from the provider side suggest that this aspect becomes especially salient during the ongoing relationship phase when IT managers need to align with the business domain to specify and prioritize change requests. However, while in the case of Client Beta the outsourcing process never reached the relationship phase, in the case of Client Alpha the business process supported by the outsourced application was a secondary process with little need for change, and in addition large parts of this process were turned over to the IT provider. This also moved the responsibility of alignment between business and IT domains pertaining to that particular function to the provider.

Our results also highlight the role of the IT Knowledge resource in form of documentation for outsourcing success. In particular, it was shown that not only the obvious types of documentation, such as source code and other forms of technical documentation are highly critical, but also documentation of operations (statistics about usage, errors and performance) and technology management (documentation of service processes and of changes to the system). Moreover, regarding this argument of outsourcing readiness, both client firms in our sample consistently and massively contributed with further supporting arguments about the importance of documentation. These findings are in line with the results of a quantitative studies showing that documentation increases a firm's propensity to outsource (Weitzel 2006) and business process outsourcing success (Wüllenweber et al. 2008).

There are of course some limitations in our findings. One limitation pertains to the depth and breadth of the case studies, which may have not uncovered all the ways by which client's IT resources may impact outsourcing success. However, presenting an exhaustive enumeration and description of all the possible ways is beyond the scope of this article. Rather, our aim in this paper is to make the point that a firm's existing IT resources may play an important, if not decisive, role in every phase of the outsourcing process and that a firm's outsourcing readiness is an issue worthy of more academic and practitioner attention.

This work represents one of the very few attempts so far to consider client's IT capabilities and resources as enablers or inhibitors for outsourcing success. We found evidence for our propositions, both from the provider's as well as from client's perspectives. This gives us confidence that the findings possess validity and reliability. Compared to the findings of Han et al. (Han et al. 2008), our qualitative analysis shows various ways by which a firm's technical and managerial IT capabilities and resources may impact the process and the outcomes of outsourcing, but also that, contingent on project particularities, not all expected effects turn out to be decisive. We conclude that future quantitative investigations need to take a more differentiated approach to investigating this relationship, on the one hand clearly distinguishing between different IT-related resources of the client at a more granular level, and on the other hand choosing different dependent variables based on the different outsourcing phases. Future research could take deeper incursions into each dimension of client's IT resource and also consider the impact of further factors like IT management processes, the alignment between business and IT domain, and their interplay, on the success of outsourcing projects. Additionally, both client organizations in our study had only *partially* outsourced their IT services. Organizations that decide to *totally* outsource their IT landscape may face fundamentally different conditions in terms of how well-prepared their IT resources are to support outsourcing. A future study may also look into this important issue.

6 References

Armenakis, A.A., Harris, S.G., and Mossholder, K.W. "Creating Readiness for Organizational Change," *Human Relations* (46:6), June 1, 1993 1993, pp 681-703.

Barthélemy, J. "The Hidden Costs of IT Outsourcing," *MIT Sloan Management Review* (42:3) 2001.

Bassellier, G., and Benbasat, I. "Business Competence of Information Technology Professionals: Conceptual Development and Influence on IT-Business Partnerships," *MIS Quarterly* (28:4) 2004, pp 673-694.

Beimborn, D., Joachim, N., and Weitzel, T. "Drivers and Inhibitors of SOA Business Value - Conceptualizing a Research Model," 14th Americas Conference on Information Systems (AMCIS), Toronto, Canada, 2008.

Bharadwaj, A.S. "A Resource-based Perspective on Information Technology Capability and Firm Performance: An Empirical Investigation," *MIS Quarterly* (24:1) 2000, pp 169-195.

Broadbent, M., Weill, P., Clair, D.S., and Kearney, A.T. "The Implications of Information Technology Infrastructure for Business Process Redesign," *MIS Quarterly* (23:2) 1999, pp 159-182.

Byrd, T.A., and Turner, D.E. "Measuring the Flexibility of Information Technology Infrastructure: Exploratory Analysis of a Construct " *Journal of Management Information Systems* (17:1) 2000, pp 167-208.

Byrd, T.A., and Turner, D.E. "An exploratory analysis of the value of the skills of IT personnel: Their relationship to IS infrastructure and competitive advantage " *Decision Sciences* (32:1) 2001a, pp 21-54.

Byrd, T.A., and Turner, D.E. "An exploratory examination of the relationship between flexible IT infrastructure and competitive advantage," *Information & Management* (39:1) 2001b, pp 41-52.

Chung, S.H., Byrd, T.A., Lewis, B.R., and Ford, F.N. "An empirical study of the relationships between IT infrastructure flexibility, mass customization, and business performance," *SIGMIS Database* (36:3) 2005, pp 26-44.

Chung, S.H., Rainer Jr., R.K., and Lewis, B.R. "The impact of information technology infrastructure flexibility on strategic alignment and application implementation," *Communications of AIS* (11) 2003, pp 191-206.

Davenport, T., and Linder, J. "Information management infrastructure: the new competitive weapon?," Proceedings of the Twenty-Seventh Hawaii International Conference on System Sciences (HICSS-27), IEEE, Hawaii, USA, 1994, pp. 885-896.

Dibbern, J. *The sourcing of application software services : empirical evidence of cultural, industry and functional differences* Physica-Verl., Heidelberg u.a., 2004, pp. XIV, 331.

Dibbern, J., Goles, T., Hirschheim, R., and Jayatilaka, B. "Information systems outsourcing: A survey and analysis of the literature," *The DATA BASE for Advances in Information Systems* (35:4) 2004, pp 6-102.

Dibbern, J., Winkler, J., and Heinzl, A. "Explaining Variations in Client Extra Costs between Software Projects Offshored to India," *MIS Quarterly* (32:2) 2008, pp 333-366.

Dubé, L., and Paré, G. "Rigor in information systems positivist case research: current practices, trends, and recommendations," *MIS Quarterly* (27:4) 2003, pp 597-635.

Duncan, N.B. "Capturing flexibility of information technology infrastructure: A study of resource characteristics and their measure," *Journal of Management Information Systems* (12:2) 1995, pp 37-57.

Eisenhardt, K.M. "Building theories from case study research," *Academy of Management Review* (14:4) 1989, pp 532-550.

Feeny, D.F., and Willcocks, L.P. "Core IS Capabilities for Exploiting Information Technology," *Sloan Management Review* (39:3) 1998, pp 9-20.

Han, H.-S., Lee, J.-N., and Seo, Y.-W. "Analyzing the impact of a firm's capability on outsourcing success: A process perspective," *Information & Management* (45:1) 2008, pp 31-42.

Ilie, V., and Parikh, M. "A Process View of Information Systems Outsourcing Research: Conceptual Gaps and Future Research Directions," 10th Americas Conference on Information Systems (AMCIS), New York, NY, USA, 2004.

Keen, P.G.W. "Information technology and the management difference: A fusion map," *IBM Systems Journal* (32:1) 1993, pp 17-39.

Lacity, M.C., Willcocks, L.P., and Feeny, D.F. "IT Outsourcing: Maximize Flexibility and Control," *Harvard Business Review* (May-June) 1995, pp 84 - 93.

Lacity, M.C., Willcocks, L.P., and Feeny, D.F. "The Value of Selective IT Sourcing," *Sloan Management Review* (37:1) 1996, pp 13-25.

Lee, J.N. "The impact of knowledge sharing, organizational capability and partnership quality on IS outsourcing success," *Information & Management* (38:5) 2001, pp 323-335.

Lei, D., and Hitt, M. "Strategic restructuring and outsourcing: The effect of mergers and acquisitions and LBOs on building firm skills and capabilities," *Journal of Management* (21:5) 1995, pp 835-859.

Loh, L., and Venkatraman, N. "Determinants of information technology outsourcing: A cross-sectional analysis," *Journal of Management Information Systems* (9:1) 1992, pp 7-24.

Martin, S.F., Wagner, H.-T., and Beimborn, D. "Process Documentation, Operational Alignment, and Flexibility in IT Outsourcing Relationships: A Knowledge-Based Perspective," International Conference on Information Systems (ICIS), Paris, France, 2008.

Nonaka, I. "A Dynamic Theory of Organizational Knowledge Creation," *Organization Science* (5:1) 1994, pp 14-37.

Peng, Y., and Wenhua, H. "A framework of total performance improvement and transaction cost-driven business process outsourcing strategy," 8th Pacific-Asia Conference on Information Systems (PACIS), Shanghai, China, 2004.

Ranganathan, C., and Balaji, S. "Critical Capabilities for Offshore Outsourcing of Information Systems," *MIS Quarterly Executive* (6:3), September 2007, pp 147-164.

Ross, J.W., Beath, C.M., and Goodhue, D.L. "Develop Long-Term Competitiveness through IT Assets," *Sloan Management Review* (38:1) 1996, pp 31-42.

Ross, J.W., and Westerman, G. "Preparing for utility computing: The role of IT architecture and relationship management," *IBM Systems Journal* (43:1) 2004, pp 5-19.

Rottman, J.W., and Lacity, M.C. "Proven Practices for Effectively Offshoring IT Work," *MIT Sloan Management Review* (47:3), Spring 2006, pp 56-63.

Schilling, M.A. "Toward a general modular systems theory and its application to interfirm product modularity," *Academy of Management Review* (25:2) 2000, pp 312-324.

Shanks, G., and Parr, A. "Positivist, Single Case Study Research in Information Systems: a Critical Analysis," in: *11th European Conference on Information Systems (ECIS 2003)*, Naples, Italy, 2003.

Todd, P.A., McKeen, J.D., and Gallupe, R.B. "The Evolution of IS Job Skills: A Content Analysis of IS Job Advertisements From 1970 to 1990," *MIS Quarterly* (19:1) 1995, pp 1-27.

Weitzel, T. "Process governance and optimization for IT Reliant Business Processes: an empirical analysis of financial processes in Germany's Fortune 1,000 non-banks," 39th Hawaii International Conference on System Sciences (HICSS-39), Hawaii, USA, 2006.

Willcocks, L., Hindle, J., Feeny, D., and Lacity, M. "IT and business process outsourcing: The knowledge potential," *Information Systems Management* (21:3) 2004, pp 7-15.

Wüllenweber, K., Beimborn, D., Weitzel, T., and König, W. "The impact of process standardization on business process outsourcing success," *Information Systems Frontiers* (10:2), April 2008, pp 211-224.

Wüllenweber, K., and Weitzel, T. "An empirical exploration of how process standardization reduces outsourcing risk," 40th Hawaii International Conference on System Sciences (HICSS40), IEEE, Hawaii, USA, 2007.

Yin, R.K. *Case study research. Design and methods*, (3rd ed.) Sage Publications, Beverly Hills, CA, 2003.

Process Documentation, Operational Alignment, and Flexibility in IT Outsourcing Relationships: A Knowledge-Based Perspective[1]

Sebastian F. Martin
E-Finance Lab
Institute for Information Systems
Goethe University, Frankfurt,
Germany
smartin@wiwi.uni-frankfurt.de

Heinz-Theo Wagner
Chair of Management and eBusiness
heilbronn business school, Germany
wagner@hn-bs.de

Daniel Beimborn
E-Finance Lab
Institute for Information Systems
Goethe University, Frankfurt, Germany
beimborn@wiwi.uni-frankfurt.de

Abstract

What is the impact of process documentation on the relationship between operational alignment and IT provider flexibility in IT outsourcing relationships? Drawing on a sample of application management outsourcing relationships from the German banking industry, we analyze the connections between interorganizational alignment of IT and business domains and IT provider flexibility. Results show that provider's tacit knowledge about the client's business domain is a strong enabler of flexibility on the provider side. If the client's business processes are poorly documented, tacit knowledge is also the main element that fosters trust, acceptance, and respect (the cognitive dimension of operational alignment) on the client side. However, when extended

---

[1] This paper has been published in the Proceedings of the International Conference on Information Systems (ICIS), Paris, France, 2008

up-to-date business process documentation is available, tacit knowledge, while still enabling flexibility, becomes irrelevant for fostering cognitive linkages between client and provider. Instead, IT provider flexibility becomes the main driver for the cognitive dimension of operational alignment.

1 Introduction

The ability of firms to dynamically reorganize resources in order to shape business strategies and customer relationships (Sambamurthy et al. 2003, p.110; Teece et al. 1997) by means of rapid reconfiguration of resources and their adjustment to changing environmental settings is essential for business success (Young-Ybarra et al. 1999). As Teece (2007, p. 1335) observes, "a key to sustained profitable growth is the ability to recombine and to reconfigure assets and organizational structures as the enterprise grows, and as markets and technologies change...". Especially in IT-intensive sectors like the financial industry, IT plays an important role for transforming business processes (Sambamurthy et al. 1997), entire firms, and their interactions with suppliers (Brynjolfsson et al. 2000). Research has found that IT may act as an enabler for business flexibility (e.g. supply chain flexibility and reconfiguration (Gosain et al. 2004; Lee et al. 2004)), for the development of new products and efficient new business processes (Farrell 2003), and for strategic agility (Weill et al. 2002) – but may also act as a barrier to change (Broadbent et al. 1999).

Over the past years, many banks have outsourced their application management activities (i.e. operations, maintenance, support, and enhancement (see Levina et al. 2003)) to third-party providers. Through outsourcing, these banks entrusted external providers with the delivery of necessary and often critical IT services, thereby becoming highly dependent on the flexibility with which the providers are able to meet their needs in dynamic and often turbulent business environments. Drawing on Evans' concept of "ex post flexibility" (Evans 1991), we refer to flexibility as the timeliness and accuracy with which providers are able to make adjustments to the managed application in response to change requests formulated by their clients.

IT providers need to be operationally aligned with their clients in order to gain and maintain the necessary understanding about the relevant technological and business process particularities of their clients that allows them to react flexibly to any change requests. Looking at *inner*-organizational settings, several authors have discussed the *link between IT business alignment and IT flexibility*. For example, Chung et al. (2003) regard flexibility as an enabler of alignment; Knoll and Jarvenpaa (1994) view flexibility as a form of alignment in turbulent environments while Duncan (1995) views alignment as both an antecedent *and* a substitute for flexibility. A positive linkage between *operational* alignment and IT flexibility has been shown by (Wagner 2007) and (Beimborn et al. 2007) who found that IT business alignment, at an operational level, had a significant positive impact on IT flexibility.

For *inter*-organizational alignment between business and IT domains, a study by Grover et al. (1996) has shown that outsourcing partnerships based on communication, trust, satisfaction, and cooperation positively impact outsourcing success. In addition to building cognitive relationships between outsourcers and providers, successful outsourcing relationships require extensive exchange of knowledge between the two parties. "This would include the transfer of knowledge about the business processes and the user information needs that are to be reflected by the software application" (Dibbern et al. 2008). For that matter, IT outsourcing relationships have been characterized as complex and knowledge-intensive relationships, requiring the integration of knowledge from different pools – i.e., business and IT domain – across firm boundaries (Dibbern et al. 2008; Tiwana 2003). In order to achieve operational alignment with their clients, IT providers may draw on *business process documentation* to understand the specifics of their client's business. However, if this kind of explicit knowledge is not available, the IT provider may have to rely on his own tacit knowledge and understanding of the client's business.

How does the availability of explicit, up-to-date process documentation influence the operational alignment between client and IT provider? How does this affect IT provider flexibility? With respect to the boundary-spanning, operational alignment between client and IT provider, despite substantial amounts of research on IT management and outsourcing relationship management, there is a twofold gap regarding

- the complex relationships between operational alignment and IT flexibility in IT outsourcing relationships and
- the role of business process documentation in shaping those relationships.

In addressing these issues, we interpret operational IT business alignment between outsourcer and IT service provider as a process of knowledge integration (compare Kearns et al. 2003) across firm boundaries and draw upon the knowledge-based theory (KBT) of the firm (Eisenhardt et al. 2002; Grant 1996a; Grant 1996b; Kogut et al. 1992) to explore the interplay between alignment dimensions and IT provider flexibility, and how knowledge integration based on up-to-date process documentation affects these links. Our research questions thus are: *What connections exist between the different dimensions of operational provider-client alignment and IT provider flexibility? How does the availability of up-to-date process documentation affect these connections?*

In order to analyze these issues, we perform a quantitative analysis on a dataset obtained from a survey carried out among Germany's largest 1,000 banks, focusing on application management outsourcing relationships between banks and IT service providers.

2 Research Background

2.1 Knowledge-based Theory

Scholars contend that "knowledge is arguably the most important asset that firms possess – a key source of both Ricardian and monopoly rents" (Liebeskind 1996, p.93). This statement reflects the importance of knowledge, which is the central tenet of the knowledge-based theory (Grant 1996a). Originating from the resource-based view (RBV) (e.g., Penrose 1959), the KBT views knowledge as the most important resource of the firm and regards knowledge integration, spanning a broad range of knowledge domains, to be the main mechanism for achieving and sustaining competitive advantage (Kogut et al. 1992).

Two forms of knowledge – explicit and tacit (Nonaka 1994) – are largely discussed in the strategic management literature. *Explicit* knowledge refers to knowledge that exists in symbolic or written form (Alavi et al. 2001). This kind of knowledge is characterized by ease of communication and transportability across individuals and organizations (Nonaka 1994). A typical example for explicit knowledge is written documentation of organizational procedures and processes (Alavi et al. 2001). In this respect, Kearns and Lederer (2000) deal with explicit knowledge in the form of IT and business plans that need to be aligned in order to achieve a fit between IT and business domains. The underlying idea hereby is that well-documented processes – i.e. systematized and formalized processes that are well understood – reduce ambiguities and thereby contribute to performance (Raymond 1990). Drawing on Nonaka (1994), this form of process documentation can be identified as *explicit business knowledge* – i.e. knowledge about the client's business domain that is available in symbolic or written form (Alavi et al. 2001).

Of course, process documentation is not the only form of documentation that may be used by the provider as a source of explicit knowledge. Technical documentation and requirements specifications, to name a few, may also be useful sources of explicit knowledge dealing with "the expressed and inferred business needs" (Tiwana et al. 2003, p.247) of the client organization. This kind of documentation may be produced for example within the requirements engineering phase of IS development projects. However, in this study we confine ourselves to process documentation, because we focus on operational alignment and flexibility during the daily operations of a business process, as opposed to IS development projects or predominantly technical specifications of IS.

In contrast to explicit knowledge, *tacit knowledge* is "rooted in action, experience, and involvement in a specific context" (Alavi et al. 2001, p.110; Nonaka 1994) and is hard to codify (Teece et al. 1997) or even "cannot be expressed in verbal, symbolic and written form" (Lee 2001, p.324). This makes its transfer across people and organizations (e.g., through apprenticeships) slow, costly, and uncertain. "An example of tacit knowledge is knowledge of the best means of approaching a particular customer – using flattery, using a hard sell, using a no-nonsense approach" (Alavi et al. 2001, p.110). The codifiable part of tacit knowledge is sometimes called *implicit* knowledge and is defined by Lee (2001, p.324) as "knowledge that can be expressed in verbal, symbolic, or written form, but has not yet been expressed". For the purpose of this paper we follow Nonaka (1994) and distinguish between explicit and tacit knowledge with tacit knowledge encompassing implicit knowledge.

Nelson and Cooprider (1996) and Reich and Benbasat (1996; 2000) developed the notion of *shared domain knowledge* which refers to the personal, *tacit knowledge* of IT and business managers about each other's domain. As we will discuss later, this construct also represents one of the most important factors of operational alignment between IT and business.

In later times, outsourcing relationships have been increasingly investigated from the perspective of knowledge-based theory (e.g., Currie 2003; Dibbern et al. 2008; Tiwana 2003). "Since each organization has its unique set of human resources, it follows that each organization possesses a unique repository of knowledge leading to knowledge asymmetry between firms" (Dibbern et al. 2008). Indeed, outsourcing relationships are typically characterized by knowledge asymmetries between client organization and outsourcing provider (Dibbern et al. 2008). Two knowledge domains, whose sources are being separated by organizational borders, need to be processed and integrated in an outsourcing relationship (Tiwana 2004). First, there is technological knowledge which usually resides on the provider side (Dibbern et al. 2008). This kind of knowledge refers to the technical skills needed to operate the outsourced IT. Second, there is knowledge about the client's business, whose source resides mainly on the client side (Dibbern et al. 2008), but which needs, to a certain degree, to be acquired by the provider in order for him to be able to provide suitable IT services. For example, if a bank outsources its credit processing system to an IT provider, the IT provider needs to acquire an understanding about how the bank is processing credit applications, in order to be able to maintain and further develop the system in a way that suites the client's needs. Using the words of Dibbern et al. (2008),

"the client continually produces new application domain knowledge which reflects its constantly changing business requirements. While it is necessary for the client to keep a certain level of technical understanding, e.g. architectural knowledge, when outsourcing an IS function to an external vendor, the majority of the technological knowledge is the responsibility of the vendor. Accordingly, [...] outsourcing brings about the challenge of integrating both types of knowledge."

This integration is not possible without a prior transfer of business process related knowledge from the client to the provider. How this transfer is being executed depends on whether the knowledge that needs to be transferred exists mainly in the form of explicit knowledge (documentation) or tacit knowledge (i.e. knowledge within the heads of individuals).

In the following, we first introduce the constructs of operational alignment and flexibility before analyzing how the prevalence of either type of knowledge (tacit vs. explicit) affects the relationship between the two constructs.

2.2 Operational IT Business Alignment

Many research contributions deal with IT business alignment as an important means for delivering business value (Avison et al. 2004; Bergeron et al. 2004; Chan et al. 2007a; Luftman et al. 2007). However, although the Strategic Alignment Model (Henderson et al. 1993) incorporates both, the *strategic* level of alignment between business and IT strategies, as well as the *operational* level of alignment between business and IT structure and processes, most research focuses on the strategic level (Bergeron et al. 2004), leaving a gap at the operational level (compare Chan et al. 2007a). Closing this gap by investigating operational IT business alignment is important for following reasons:

- Strategy needs to be transformed into "daily business" (Gordon et al. 2000), because "strategies are only effective when they are translated into actions readily" (Feurer et al. 2000, p.23), so that "one's strategy gets enacted" at the operational level (Chan et al. 2007a, p. 47).

- "The ability to translate the business strategy into processes, IS investments and change plans that match the business priorities" as well as "the ability to translate the business strategy into long term information architectures, technology infrastructure and resourcing plans that enable the implementation of the strategy" (Peppard et al. 2004, p.176) are essential capabilities.

- "Lower-level functioning groups need to interact in order to transform strategy into daily business" (Gordon et al. 2000, p.6).

- The operational level of alignment dealing with functional integration rather than with strategic integration is more appropriate for process-level research, which is in the focus of this research.

Drawing on the social dimension of alignment from (Reich et al. 1996) and based on (Nelson et al. 1996), (Reich et al. 2000) as well as (Tiwana et al. 2003), Wagner (2007) has developed an *operational* alignment construct for process-level research focusing on "run the business" rather than on projects, which differ from daily business in that they require a dedicated budget, a project manager, and a project team. He points out three distinct dimensions of operational alignment, *which we will consider in the following*: *shared knowledge*, *cognitive relationship*, and *communication*.

Shared knowledge has previously been shown to be an essential predictor of IS performance (Nelson et al. 1996). It is needed for successful knowledge integration (Kearns et al. 2006) and is termed a key takeaway for practitioners by literature pointing to the importance of sharing knowledge (Chan et al. 2007b). Moreover, "only shared domain knowledge unambiguously distinguishes high from low achievers" over the long term (Avison et al. 2004, p.229). Shared knowledge refers to both "IT-knowledgeable business managers and business-knowledgeable IT managers" (Reich et al. 2000, p.84), is bound to individuals and thus may be regarded as a form of *tacit knowledge* (Nonaka 1994) – i.e. knowledge that is not codified, representing "the ability of IT and business executives, at a deep level, to understand and be able to participate in the others' key processes and to respect each other's unique contribution and challenges" (Reich et al. 2000, p.86). This perspective is supported by Nelson and Cooprider's (1996, p.411) definition of shared knowledge as individual-related "understanding and appreciation among IS and line managers for the technologies and processes that affect their mutual performance". For the purpose of this paper, we adopt a unilateral view on shared knowledge in that we are regarding only one aspect of this dimension, namely the business knowledge of the IT professionals (Bassellier et al. 2004). Therefore, in the following we refer to shared knowledge as *tacit cross-domain knowledge of IT provider employees* about the client firm's business domain.

The second component of operational alignment, *cognitive relationship*, may be seen as both influencing the development of shared knowledge as well as being influenced by shared knowledge (Hansen 1999; Tiwana et al. 2003). Cognitive relationship encompasses concepts like trust, mutual respect, mutual acceptance, and mutual understanding of common goals – elements which form the critical foundation of a good relationship between IT and business people (Galunic et al. 1998; Nelson et al. 1996; Tiwana et al. 2003), regardless of whether both domains are located within or across the confines of a single firm or not. In both cases, high degrees of mutual respect and understanding are reflective for a successful relationship between IT and business domain, as perceived by the client.

Finally, *communication* underlies cognitive relationships and the development of shared knowledge, providing the structural linkage by means of which knowledge can be shared easily (Alavi et al. 2001; Tiwana 2003) and tightening cognitive relationships through frequent interaction (Tiwana et al. 2003). Communication refers to the kind and quality of interaction patterns and communication channels between the representatives of IT and business domains in the daily business, encompassing, for example, routines established to enable the process of joint knowledge creation (Reich et al. 2000; Tiwana et al. 2003).

2.3 IT Provider Flexibility

IT plays a significant role in ensuring a firm's ability to readjust and reconfigure its resources and business processes to match dynamically changing market demands (Byrd et al. 2000). In business environments characterized by uncertainty and constant change, flexibility is a critical aspect of success (Young-Ybarra et al. 1999) and a main component of IT service quality, as perceived by the service recipient (Kettinger et al. 1997). In this research, we refer to IT flexibility as an ex-post maneuver in the sense of Evans, who defines this kind of flexibility as "after-the-fact adjustments undertaken once a triggering episode has occurred" (Evans 1991, p.75). In the context of IT outsourcing relationships, investigated in this paper, the triggering episode for the adjustments to be undertaken is represented by change requests posed by the client firm to the IT provider. The flexibility of the IT provider is reflected by the timeliness and accuracy with which the provider reacts to such requests, implementing the IT change.

3 Research Model

Our research model (Figure 1) depicts the hypothesized links between operational alignment (shared knowledge, communication, and cognition), IT provider flexibility, and process documentation which we will discuss in detail in the following section.

In IT outsourcing relationships, operational alignment between the IT domain and the business domain is achieved through knowledge transfer and integration between business client and IT provider. Frequent interaction enhances the transfer of knowledge, thus facilitating knowledge sharing (Alavi et al. 2001; Tiwana 2003) between IT and business domain (Reich et al. 1996; Tiwana et al. 2003) and also leads to tight cognitive linkages between the members of both domains (Tiwana et al. 2003). As mentioned above, cognitive linkages refer to trust, respect, acceptance, as well as shared mutual understanding of collective goals, business strategies, organizational work processes, and the work environment among business domain (the banking client) and IT domain (the IT provider). Constant transfer of knowledge between client and provider is only possible with frequent interaction – i.e., transferring knowledge through formal and informal communication. Through this interaction, both shared domain knowledge and cognitive linkages are increasing (Alavi et al. 2001; Galunic et al. 1998; Hansen 1999). For the operational alignment dimensions, this means that communication is an antecedent of both shared knowledge as well as cognition. Thus, our first two hypotheses are:

H1: Frequent communication is associated with higher degrees of shared knowledge.

H2: Frequent communication is associated with higher degrees of cognition.

Shared knowledge is important for the coordination among different agents who have different models of the world (Foss 1999). Thus, shared knowledge forms the basis for aligned actions, because it provides the IT domain with the business knowledge necessary to provide effective services for the business side. In IT outsourcing relationships, customer insight affects the timeliness and accuracy with which the provider firm reacts to its client's change requests. The more the IT provider understands the specifics of his clients' business and internal processes, the more likely it is that he will be able to react flexible and knowledgeable to change requests (Wagner 2007). We therefore hypothesize that

H3: Shared knowledge positively influences IT provider flexibility.

The availability of explicit, formal documentation (Grover et al. 2005) is an important indication of organizational maturity and increases efficiency by reducing ambiguities (Dewett et al. 2001). If explicit knowledge (in form of an up-to-date documentation) about the client's business processes which are supported by the outsourced application is not available, the only sources of information to which the provider can resort when implementing a change are the provider's own tacit knowledge about the business specifics of the client and the tacit knowledge incorporated in the client's personnel. By contrast, if explicit knowledge is available in form of up-to-date documentation, the information needed by the provider for quick and accurate reaction to client demands can be acquired by referring to this documentation. In this case, shared (tacit) knowledge is an important complement to explicit knowledge but not the only source of information. Therefore, we hypothesize:

H4: When up-to-date business process documentation is available, shared knowledge loses importance for IT provider flexibility.

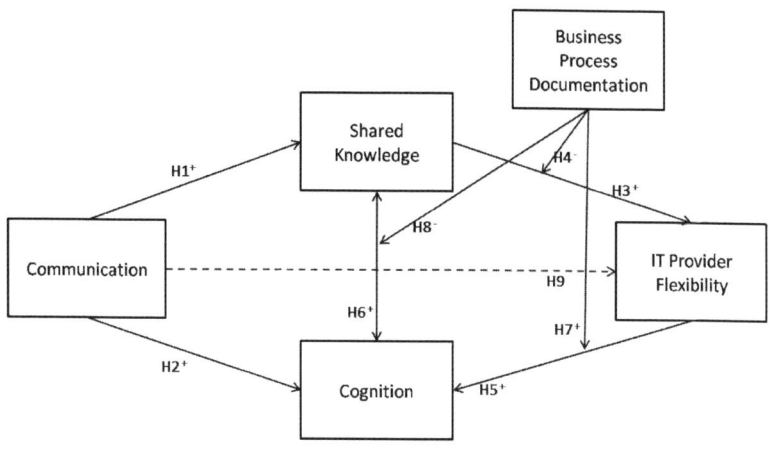

Figure 1: Research Model

Alignment can increase responsiveness to a changing environment as well as to user requests and requirements, regarding the IS as a means to preserve the relationship between the business and the IT domain (Young-Ybarra et al. 1999). This consideration is based on the concept of balanced asset specificity and resembles cognitive linkages between IT and business as it refers to a balanced dependence between the two domains as a collective incentive to maintain the relationship (Young-Ybarra et al. 1999). The reason for this increased responsiveness is that failing to meet business needs by not being fast enough to correct errors or implement changes requested by the business side may result in damaging the relationship between IT and business domain which has been created over time and which is seen as an asset by both sides (Wagner 2007) because it is essential for the success of the relationship. This reasoning holds especially true when there is a client-provider relationship between business and IT domains, as it is the case in IT outsourcing relationships. Therefore, we hypothesize that

H5: IT provider flexibility has a positive influence on cognition.

Cognitive linkages may be seen as both a driver as well as an outcome of shared knowledge (Hansen 1999; Tiwana et al. 2003). In support of the positive influence of cognition on shared knowledge one may argue that, once cognitive linkages (e.g. referring to mutual trust) are established, the willingness to share knowledge may increase. At the side of the receiver of knowledge, established cognitive linkages may also increase the willingness to *accept* knowledge. Thus cognitive linkages facilitate knowledge sharing. This is in line with the study of Nelson and Cooprider (1996) who show that mutual trust and mutual influence positively impact shared knowledge by alleviating barriers to cooperation and creating a common frame of reference. On the other hand, in support of the inverse effect (shared knowledge on cognition), one may argue that the provider's knowledge about the clients' business domain enables him to "speak the client's language". This ability may rouse acceptance and respect on the client's side, thus acting as an enabler for cognitive linkages. This assertion is supported by Bassellier and Benbasat (2004) who found that IT professionals have a greater intention to develop and strengthen relationships when they reach higher levels of business knowledge. Thus, the relationship between the two constructs resembles a spiral, where shared knowledge rouses cognition and cognition rouses the willingness to accept and internalize information stemming from the other party, which translates into higher levels of shared knowledge. However, regardless of the direction of influence, we deem that the relationship between the two constructs is a positive one, since in both cases higher levels of one construct are associated with higher levels of the other construct. Therefore we hypothesize:

H6: There is a positive relationship between shared knowledge and cognition.

The earlier hypothesized positive link between flexibility and cognition may be even stronger when explicit knowledge in form of extensive up-to-date documentation is made available to the provider. The reason is that the client may now be more demanding since, from his point of view, all information needed by the provider for timely and accurate reaction is now available in explicit form. On the other hand, merely "speaking the customer's language" will not be enough anymore to gain the client's trust and respect. When all information needed for providing flexible services is available, then the provider really needs to "start delivering" rather than just showing business domain knowledge. Therefore, we hypothesize that

H7: When up-to-date business process documentation is available, IT provider flexibility gains importance for cognition.

H8: When up-to-date business process documentation is available, shared knowledge loses importance for cognition.

Communication relies on formal and informal communication channels and is thus important for knowledge transfer and the development of cognitive linkages. In order to influence IT provider flexibility, it is necessary to transfer content (i.e., knowledge and cognition). This is supported by Tiwana et al. (2003) who found business-IS linkages to be an antecedent of knowledge integration with no direct effect on their dependent variable IS development capability. Therefore we hypothesize that communication per se hardly impacts IT provider flexibility.

H9: Communication has a negligible direct impact on IT provider flexibility.

4 Methodology

This study uses a dataset obtained from a survey carried out in 2005 among Germany's top 1,000 banks (according to total assets). Main focus of the survey was to investigate the role of IT for process performance in the corporate (SME) loans business and to identify critical drivers of effective IT usage. The questionnaire was answered by the chief credit officers of 136 banks, resulting in a response rate of 13.6%. The sample is statistically representative regarding firm size (assets). From the total of 136 received questionnaires, a number of 104 respondents indicated that their credit processing system – which was the IT system that all respondents were asked to refer to when answering the questionnaire – is externally managed and run by an outsourcing provider (compared to 20 banks stating to use an in-house system and 12 respondents who gave no answer). 73 out of them were usable since they showed no missing values in the applied items.

Construct	Item	Indicator	References
Cognition	COG1	There exists a lot of mutual trust and respect between IT unit and business unit.	(Bhatt 2003; Luftman 2003; Ravichandran et al. 2005; Teo et al. 1999)
	COG2	The IT unit and the business unit regularly consult each other.	(Bhatt 2003; Broadbent et al. 1993; Chung et al. 2003; Ravichandran et al. 2005; Reich et al. 1996)
	COG3	A change to the IS is implemented in close interaction between business unit and IT unit.	(Bergeron et al. 2004; Broadbent et al. 1993; Chung et al. 2003; Reich et al. 1996; Segars et al. 1998)
Communication	COMM1	There are meetings on a regular basis between IT unit and business unit to control change processes.	(Broadbent et al. 1993; Chung et al. 2003; Reich et al. 1996)
	COMM2	There are meetings on a regular basis between IT unit and business unit for business process improvements.	(Broadbent et al. 1993; Chung et al. 2003; Reich et al. 1996)
	COMM3	There exist meetings on a regular basis between IT unit and business unit to ensure an effective and efficient change process.	(Broadbent et al. 1993; Chung et al. 2003; Reich et al. 1996)
IT Provider Flexibility	FLEX1	If there are critical bugs in the IT applications, they get fixed in a timely manner.	(Byrd et al. 2001)
	FLEX2	If there are non-critical bugs in the IT applications, they get fixed in a timely manner.	(Byrd et al. 2001)
	FLEX3	The IT unit reacts flexible to change requests from the business unit.	(Young-Ybarra et al. 1999)
	FLEX4	The IT unit realizes change requests from the business unit in appropriate time.	(Young-Ybarra et al. 1999)
	FLEX5	The IT unit is very responsive regarding needs of the business unit.	(Chang et al. 2005; Segars et al. 1998; Teo et al. 1999)
Shared Knowledge	SK1	The employees of the IT unit are able to interpret business-related problems and to develop solutions.	(Bhatt 2003; Broadbent et al. 1993; Ravichandran et al. 2005; Reich et al. 1996; Segars et al. 1998; Teo et al. 1999)
	SK2	The employees of the IT unit know the SME credit business process.	(Bhatt 2003; Boynton et al. 1994; Broadbent et al. 1993; Reich et al. 1996; Teo et al. 1999; Teo et al. 1997)
	SK3	The IT unit implements change requests according to the requirements of the business unit.	(Broadbent et al. 1993; Chang et al. 2005; Reich et al. 1996)

Table 1: Construct specification (original questionnaire was provided in German)

We chose to focus on the German banking sector for several reasons. First, banks employ especially IT-intensive processes, since this is, beside people, their only production resource. Second, high and frequently changing regulations as well as high competition inter alia resulting from quite homogenous products require them to have a highly flexible IT infrastructure and information systems. Third, banks in Germany have usually outsourced the operations and maintenance of their IT/IS. The German banking industry features a particular structure as more than 80% of all German banks are public savings banks or credit cooperatives. Both the credit cooperatives and the public savings banks are organized in quite tight national associations and have founded joint data processing centers in the 70ies or even earlier. Thus, many German banks have never operated their IT internally.

As an important side effect, the choice of just one industry and just one business process avoids heterogeneity. This makes the use of several demographic control variables obsolete (see Chiasson et al. 2005) because we focus on similar IT systems, on similar business contexts, on people with comparable backgrounds and on firms acting in the same regulatory environment and in comparable customer segments. We focus on a primary business process (i.e. the process for granting and managing investment loans to small and medium-sized enterprises or – short – the SME credit process) and its underlying IT application because following Barua et al. (1995), we believe that variance at the aggregation level of a firm will dilute and disguise IT impacts. This can be avoided by focusing on only one core process. Therefore, all constructs are operationalized at the business process level. As suggested by Eisenhardt (1989), the indicator questions have been derived mainly from validated scales from the literature and were adapted to our purpose. This is especially true for operational IT business alignment based on the described set of three dimensions, as research on this issue is very rare.

For conducting the statistical analysis, we used Partial Least Square (PLS) employing SmartPLS 2.0 (Ringle et al. 2005). PLS was chosen for two reasons. First, PLS is more appropriate if theory is untested in an application domain or tentative (Gopal et al. 1993), and second, our data set predominantly consists of not normally distributed variables, which prevents the use of covariance-based instruments. For testing the model, we used only reflective measures (listed in Table 1).

The effect of process documentation on the links between shared knowledge, cognition, and flexibility (H4, H7, and H8) was tested by conducting a group comparison. We divided the sample into two groups of banks with low vs. high process documentation and performed 2000 bootstraps of the PLS model with each sub sample. The group comparison was done both by a Mann-Whitney test and a T-test on the resulting path coefficients.

5 Results

5.1 Reliability and Validity

This section deals with the statistical validity and reliability of the constructs and their linkages, as well as potential biases and the validity of the mapping between items and constructs. First, non-response bias and common method bias are discussed. Then, the validity and reliability of the PLS measurement model are investigated, including content and construct validity.

5.1.1 Non-Response Bias and Common Method Bias

To test for non-response bias, we distinguished between respondents and late respondents (managers who responded after a reminder (Worren et al. 2002)). Following Kearns and Lederer (2004), the late respondents (52.2% of all respondents) were treated as non-respondents, because they share similarities with non-respondents. We found no significant differences, indicating that non-response bias cannot be assumed.

Common method bias may occur when a single source is being used for assessing both the independent as well as the dependent constructs. Podsakoff et al. (2003) distinguish between procedural and statistical remedies to cope with common method bias. The procedural remedies refer to measures carried out before data collection and are related to the design of the questionnaire. The statistical remedies are tests after data collection. To address procedural remedies we removed ambiguous and complex items from the questionnaire by using pre-tests; reverse-coded items were used to counter acquiescence effects, and anonymity of respondents was assured to counter social desirability effects. To address statistical remedies, we used Harman's factor test (Podsakoff et al. 1986) that showed no single factor accounting for the majority of variance. Moreover, we followed the approach described by Liang et al. (2007) by allowing the items to load both on their construct (via single-item constructs) and on a latent common methods factor in order to verify that the common methods factor does not provide a substantial explanation of the variance compared to the original latent variable.

5.1.2 PLS Measurement Model

Content validity refers to the extent to which measures reflect the intended meaning of a construct (Zhu et al. 2002). Content validity was assured by deriving indicator questions from prior research and by implementing pre-tests to test for ambiguities. The insights from the pre-tests were used to adapt single indicator questions to the intended meaning, or to remove them from the questionnaire at all if those items were too complex.

Indicator reliability deals with the statistical fit between an indicator and its corresponding latent variable. Loadings of the indicator to their respective construct must not be below 0.5 and should be above the recommended threshold of 0.707 (Hulland 1999). Loadings between 0.5 and 0.707 can be accepted if all other items belonging to a certain construct are above 0.707 (Chin 1998). Using the PLS bootstrap resampling we created 500 random samples of our data set to test the stability and statistical significance of the estimated constructs (Chin 1998). The resulting T-values from the t-statistics represent the level of significance for each single item. In the model tested, all loadings of the indicators are above the recommended 0.707 parameter value except in two cases (see Table 2) and significant at the 0.01 level, demonstrating indicator reliability.

Construct	Indicator	Total sample	Group with low process documentation	Group with high process documentation
Cognition	COG1	.737**	.740**	.770**
	COG2	.737**	.675**	.777**
	COG3	.844**	.853**	.807**
Communication	COMM1	.908**	.838**	.928**
	COMM2	.937**	.978**	.930**
	COMM3	.953**	.909**	.974**
IT Provider Flexibility	FLEX1	.780**	.720**	.749**
	FLEX2	.771**	.824**	.715**
	FLEX3	.814**	.796**	.747**
	FLEX4	.836**	.771**	.839**
	FLEX5	.714**	.853**	.816**
Shared Knowledge	SK1	.808**	.849**	.754**
	SK2	.708**	.857**	.575*
	SK3	.828**	.701**	.891**

Table 2: Loadings (**: p<.01, *: p<.05)

Construct validity is composed of convergent and discriminant validity and deals with the accuracy by which the measures actually describe the construct (Gefen et al. 2005). *Convergent validity* refers to the internal consistency of the set of items and is analyzed by calculating the Average Variance Extracted (AVE) and the composite reliability. It is recommended to have an AVE greater than 0.5 (Chin 1998) and a composite reliability of greater than 0.7 (Nunnally 1978). Composite reliability is comparable to Cronbach's Alpha that is also depicted in Table 3 (and in Table 9 for the sub-samples, together with the single

R square values) demonstrating that our model exhibits a good correlation between the indicators and their construct.

	Composite Reliability	AVE	Cronbach's Alpha	R Square
Cognition	.818	.600	.672	.435
Communication	.952	.870	.925	
IT Provider Flexibility	.888	.615	.845	.338
Shared Knowledge	.826	.613	.726	.019

Table 3: Quality Measures for Latent Variables (Results from sub-samples are presented in the appendix)

	Cognition	Communication	IT Provider Flexibility	Shared Knowledge
Cognition	.775			
Communication	.295	.933		
IT Provider Flexibility	.619	.151	.784	
Shared Knowledge	.452	.138	.577	.783

Table 4: Correlations of Latent Variables and AVE Square Root (Shaded Cells) (Results from sub-samples are presented in the appendix)

Indicator	Cognition	Communication	IT Provider Flexibility	Shared Knowledge
COG1	.737	.002	.547	.389
COG2	.737	.221	.335	.315
COG3	.844	.403	.539	.355
COMM1	.265	.908	.110	.102
COMM2	.247	.937	.145	.159
COMM3	.310	.953	.162	.123
FLEX1	.506	.208	.780	.474
FLEX2	.329	-.040	.771	.332
FLEX3	.430	.204	.814	.560
FLEX4	.424	.152	.836	.462
FLEX5	.684	-.022	.714	.369
SK1	.366	.044	.325	.808
SK2	.232	.0430	.234	.708
SK3	.411	.178	.635	.828

Table 5: Cross Loadings of Manifest Variables

Discriminant validity is concerned with whether the construct, measured by the set of items, is discriminant from other constructs. As shown by Tables 4 and 10 show (see appendix for Table 10), all correlations between the constructs are lower than the square root of the average variance extracted (presented in the diagonal). Together with Table 5, which shows that the indicators load more strongly on their respective construct than on any other construct, this demonstrates a sufficient statistical separation between the different sets of indicators (Gefen et al. 2000).

Summarizing the results, each construct showed the required internal consistency, convergent validity, and discriminant validity. The next section copes with the results of testing our research model.

5.2 Structural Model and Group Comparison

Figure 2 shows the PLS results for the total sample. For deriving the t-values and the resulting significance levels, we used the bootstrapping procedure with 500 sub-samples (Chin 1998). The results are also depicted in Figure 2.

As a result, we find weakly significant paths from communication to shared knowledge and from shared knowledge to cognition. The paths related with IT provider flexibility are highly significant (shared knowledge → IT provider flexibility (H3), IT provider flexibility → cognition (H5)) and the positive relationship between communication and cognition (H2) is significant as well. By contrast, the direct link from communication to IT provider flexibility is, as proposed above (H9), non-existent.

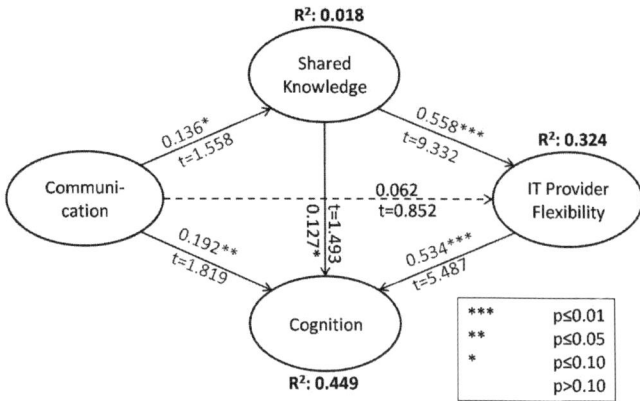

Figure 2: PLS Results – Complete Sample (n = 73)

In order to analyze the moderating effect of process documentation, the data set was divided into two groups, based on the level of high-quality, up-to-date documentation available for the SME credit process. The first group contained datasets in which the respondents indicated low and medium levels of high-quality process documentation (39 cases). The second group contained cases with high and very high levels of high-quality process documentation (58 cases). The remaining 7 respondents gave no answer about the level of documentation and therefore these datasets had to be excluded from the analysis. Moreover, missing values led to a reduction of the data sets to 30 and 43 cases in the two groups.

The actual group comparison of the path coefficients is based on a bootstrapping with 500 samples. The distributions of path coefficients between both groups were compared by applying the Mann-Whitney test and the T-test, which both showed consistent results. All path coefficients differ significantly between the two samples, but in different strength and direction. The validity and reliability criteria for the PLS results from testing the model with the two groups are presented in Table 9 in the appendix.

Path	Original path coefficient (T-value)		Average path coefficient from 2000 bootstraps (std. dev.)		Mann-Whitney test on group difference	T-test on pair-wise difference ≠ 0
	Low process documentation (n_{low} = 30)	High process documentation (n_{high} = 43)	Low process documentation (n_{low}=30)	High process documentation (n_{high}=43)	(Z, p)	(T, p)
Shared Knowledge → IT Provider Flexibility	.668 (5.16)	.546 (5.41)	.679 (.108)	.569 (.101)	(-35.5, .000)	(-33.0, .000)
IT Provider Flexibility → Cognition	.254 (1.53)	.648 (5.72)	.306 (.165)	.637 (.113)	(-49.6, .000)	(-74.7, .000)
Shared Knowledge → Cognition	.404 (2.28)	.036 (.32)	.383 (.177)	.051 (.114)	(-48.8, .000)	(-71.3, .000)

Table 6: Group Comparison of Path Coefficients (Test of H4, H7, H8)

Hypothesis	Result
H1: Frequent communication is associated with higher degrees of shared knowledge.	Weakly supported
H2: Frequent communication is associated with higher degrees of cognition.	Supported
H3: Shared knowledge positively influences IT provider flexibility.	Strongly supported
H4: When up-to-date business process documentation is available, shared knowledge loses importance for IT provider flexibility.	Weakly supported
H5: IT provider flexibility has a positive influence on cognition.	Strongly supported
H6: There is a positive relationship between shared knowledge and cognition.	Weakly supported
H7: When up-to-date business process documentation is available, flexibility gains importance for cognition.	Supported
H8: When up-to-date business process documentation is available, shared (tacit) knowledge loses importance for cognition.	Supported
H9: Communication has a negligible direct impact on IT provider flexibility	Supported

Table 7: Summary of the Results

As Table 6 shows, the relationship between shared knowledge and cognition is much stronger in the low-documentation group and becomes, compared to the high-documentation group and to the overall sample, highly significant. Consequently, H8 is strongly confirmed. Inversely, the impact of IT provider flexibility on the outsourcer's cognition is much higher in the high-documentation group but becomes insignificant in the low-documentation group (confirming H7). Less difference can be found regarding the relationship between shared knowledge and IT provider flexibility; the low-process documentation group shows only slightly higher path coefficients for this relationship, weakly supporting H4. Table 7 summarizes the overall results.

6 Discussion and Limitations

As hypothesized, the link between shared knowledge and cognition became weaker in the presence of good process documentation (H8) – in fact, the influence of the IT provider's cross-domain knowledge on cognition even became insignificant in the sample featuring extended process documentation. We also tested the total effects of shared knowledge on cognition (incorporating both the direct relationship and also the one which is mediated by IT provider flexibility) and found, as an overall effect, a significant decrease in this relationship. This supports our reasoning that, in the case of low levels of documentation, the provider has the chance to create a good impression and gain the client's respect and acceptance by proving to be knowledgeable about the client's business domain. This may be so because in order to overcome the shortcoming of not having reliable documentation to draw upon, both parties – outsourcer and IT provider – have to fully concentrate on explicating, transferring, and integrating tacit knowledge by writing documents, practicing of procedures, coaching, and mentoring. The predominant direction of knowledge transfer is from the outsourcer to the IT service provider. The ease with which the provider assimilates knowledge about the client's business procedures, information systems requirements, etc. – which is directly enabled by the amount of business domain knowledge possessed by the provider – creates the proper climate for strong cognitive relationships.

However, if up-to-date documentation is available, the influence of the provider's tacit business domain knowledge on the cognitive relationship decreases significantly as the client now becomes more demanding, expecting from the provider to "start delivering", instead of only proving to be knowledgeable about the client's domain. Flexibility on the provider side proves to be a highly relevant aspect of service quality as perceived by the client (compare Kettinger et al. 1997). This development is supported by the highly significant difference between the flexibility-cognition relationships within the two groups.

A bit unexpectedly, the impact of shared knowledge on IT provider flexibility – although significantly reduced compared to the group with low documentation – still remains strong when up-to-date documentation is available. The reason for this might be that explicit documentation, although it represents a valuable additional source of information, is not a complete substitute for personal domain knowledge. In the presence of up-to-date documentation, the basis for delivering flexible services may be enhanced by explicit, codified information, but the tacit knowledge of the provider's employees, which is mainly based on experience, continues to be an important driver (compare Alavi et al. 2001).

Our approach involves several limitations. First, we used business executives' perceptions as a proxy for IT provider flexibility which may cause a bias. However, the use of business executives' perceptions is widely accepted in IS research (Bergeron et al. 2004; Chan et al. 1997; Cragg et al. 2002), because there is evidence in literature that they correlate with objective measures. As Tallon and Kraemer (2007, p.19) put it regarding IT value research: "Perceptions may therefore not be entirely accurate, but, in the subconscious reasoning of executives who are trying to give a reasoned response to the question of IT value, it is accurate enough". Moreover, the business executives represent the users of the system and are, therefore, the *relevant* source for evaluating IT provider flexibility from the client's perspective.

Second, we have only used a single person to capture an organizational perspective. This limitation was relaxed by addressing the expert in charge of the credit process to get the relevant variables (Tallon et al. 2000) and by accompanying the survey by a set of case studies that allowed balancing the view of the manager in charge with other manager's views where we did not find great deviations in the assessment.

Third, the generalizability of results suffers from the single-person and single-point-in-time measurement (threat of method bias) as well as from the focus on only one industry. However, this narrow focus may also be seen as strength of our study, because it excludes much of the potential side-effects from uncontrolled variables that might occur in a wider frameset.

Fourth, for the group comparison, we had only quite small samples. Particularly, the low-documentation sample was comparably low, since the banking industry has caught up regarding the level of process documentation, also due to regulatory requirements, leaving only few banks behind. The small samples did not allow for a group comparison regarding construct levels (i.e. average levels of latent variable scores) in order to see whether the levels of shared knowledge, flexibility, and cognition themselves differed between banks with low vs. high process documentation. Due to the small sample sizes, we only found insignificant results. In the future, we will try to gather comparable data from other industries in order to put our findings onto a broader statistical basis.

7 Conclusion

The aim of this study was to explore the interplay of the different dimensions of operational alignment with IT provider flexibility in the context of IT outsourcing relationships and the moderating role of process documentation in affecting this interplay. Table 8 summarizes the contributions of this paper with regard to our research questions and the implications of our findings for theory and practice.

Research Question	Main Contribution to Theory	Implications for Practice
What connections exist between the different alignment dimensions and IT provider flexibility?	We could demonstrate a strong influence of shared knowledge on IT provider flexibility and a strong influence of IT provider flexibility on cognition. As expected, the third dimension of operational alignment (communication) does not have a direct effect on flexibility. Instead, its effect on flexibility is mediated by shared knowledge.	First of all, management should foster knowledge exchange between the client and the IT service provider because it promotes the development of business understanding and orientation which helps the IT service provider to provide flexible services. This can be done by a) mentoring and on-the-job-training of IT service provider employees through dedicated client personnel; b) fostering communication by means of formal meetings and up-to-date documentation.
How does the availability of process documentation affect these connections?	In the presence of up-to-date process documentation, the link between shared knowledge and cognition is weaker than it is when the level of documentation is low. Furthermore, the influence of IT provider's cross-domain tacit knowledge on cognition is highly significant when there is little explicit knowledge in form of up-to date-documentation. This link becomes insignificant when high levels of explicit knowledge in form of process documentation are employed.	While good process documentation enhances the client organization's outsourcing readiness by fostering knowledge transferability, bank management should be aware that tacit knowledge is also important for IT provider flexibility even in cases where a comprehensive and up-to-date documentation is available. Therefore, banks and their IT providers should not only focus on a perfect documentation (e.g. process description, service level agreements), which certainly is necessary, but also on facilitating the exchange of procedural knowledge between the two domains.

Table 8: Summary of Theoretical and Managerial Contributions

In conclusion, we find that business process documentation plays a subtle role in shaping the relationship between IT providers and their banking clients. This is demonstrated by the unexpectedly strong negative effect of documentation on the link between shared knowledge and cognition (which practically vanishes in the prevalence of good-quality, up-to-date business process documentation), but also on the link between IT flexibility and cognition, which only becomes significant when up-to-date documentation is available.

As stated in the Research Background section, process documentation is not the only source of explicit knowledge about the client's specifics the provider may draw upon. It may be worthwhile for future research to tackle the question how other kinds of documentation – like technical documentation, job descriptions, or requirements specifications – affect the relationship between clients and IT providers. Future research should also analyze to what extent the effort of keeping a detailed, up-to-date documentation contributes to achieving performance in outsourcing outcomes like relationship quality and service quality.

8 Acknowledgement

This work was developed as part of a research project of the E-Finance Lab, Frankfurt am Main, Germany (www.efinancelab.com). We are indebted to the participating universities and industry partners.

9 References

Alavi, M., and Leidner, D.E. "Review: Knowledge Management and Knowledge Management Systems: Conceptual Foundations and Research Issues," *MIS Quarterly* (25:1) 2001, pp 107-136.

Avison, D., Jones, J., Powell, P., and Wilson, D. "Using and Validating the Strategic Alignment Model," *Journal of Strategic Information Systems* (13:3) 2004, pp 223-246.

Barua, A., Kriebel, C.H., and Mukhopadhyay, T. "Information Technologies and Business Value: An Analytical and Empirical Investigation," *Information Systems Research* (6:1) 1995, pp 3-23.

Bassellier, G., and Benbasat, I. "Business Competence of Information Technology Professionals: Conceptual Development and Influence on IT-Business Partnerships," *MIS Quarterly* (28:4) 2004, pp 673-694.

Beimborn, D., Franke, J., Wagner, H.-T., and Weitzel, T. "The Impact of Operational Alignment on IT Flexibility - Empirical Evidence from a Survey in the German Banking Industry," 13th Americas Conference on Information Systems (AMCIS 2007), Keystone (CO), USA, 2007.

Bergeron, F., Raymond, L., and Rivard, S. "Ideal patterns of strategic alignment and business performance," *Information & Management* (41:8) 2004, pp 1003-1020.

Bhatt, G.D. "Managing Information Systems Competence for Competitive Advantage: An Empirical Analysis," Proceedings of the 24th International Conference on Information Systems, Seattle, Washington, USA, 2003, pp. 134-142.

Boynton, A.C., Zmud, R.W., and Jacobs, G.C. "The Influence of IT Management Practice on IT Use in Large Organizations," *MIS Quarterly* (18:3) 1994, pp 299-318.

Broadbent, M., and Weill, P. "Improving business and information strategy alignment: Learning from the banking industry," *IBM Systems Journal* (32:1) 1993, pp 162-179.

Broadbent, M., Weill, P., and Neo, B.S. "Strategic context and patterns of IT infrastructure capabilities," *Journal of Strategic Information Systems* (8:2) 1999, pp 157-187.

Brynjolfsson, E., and Hitt, L.M. "Beyond Computation: Information Technology, Organizational Transformation and Business Performance," *Journal of Economic Perspectives* (14:4) 2000, pp 23-48.

Byrd, T.A., and Turner, D.E. "Measuring the flexibility of information technology infrastructure: exploratory analysis of a construct," *Journal of Management Information Systems* (17:1) 2000, pp 167-208.

Byrd, T.A., and Turner, D.E. "An exploratory examination of the relationship between IT infrastructure and competitive advantage," *Information & Management* (39:1) 2001, pp 41-52.

Chan, Y.E., Huff, S.L., Barclay, D.W., and Copeland, D.G. "Business Strategic Orientation, Information Systems Strategic Orientation, and Strategic Alignment," *Information Systems Research* (8:2) 1997, pp 125-150.

Chan, Y.E., and Reich, B.H. "IT alignment: an annotated bibliography," *Journal of Information Technology* (22:2) 2007a, pp 316-396.

Chan, Y.E., and Reich, B.H. "IT alignment: what have we learned?," *Journal of Information Technology* (22:2) 2007b, pp 297-315.

Chang, J.C.-J., and King, W.R. "Measuring the Performance of Information Systems: A Functional Scorecard," *Journal of Management Information Systems* (22:1) 2005, pp 85-115.

Chiasson, M.W., and Davidson, E. "Taking Industry Seriously in Information Systems Research," *MIS Quarterly* (29:4) 2005, pp 591-605.

Chin, W.W. "The Partial Least Square Approach to Structural Equation Modeling," in: *Modern Methods for Business Research,* G.A. Marcoulides (ed.), Lawrence Erlbaum Associates, Mahwah, NJ, USA, 1998, pp. 295-336.

Chung, S.H., Rainer, R.K., and Lewis, B.R. "The Impact of Information Technology Infrastructure Flexibility on Strategic Alignment and Applications Implementation," *Communications of the Association for Information Systems* (11) 2003, pp 191-206.

Cragg, P., King, M., and Hussin, H. "IT alignment and firm performance in small manufacturing firms," *Journal of Strategic Information Systems* (11:2) 2002, pp 109-132.

Currie, W.L. "A knowledge-based risk assessment framework for evaluating web-enabled application outsourcing projects," *International Journal of Project Management* (21:3) 2003, pp 207-217.

Dewett, T., and Jones, G.R. "The role of information technology in the organization: a review, model, and assessment," *Journal of Management* (27:3) 2001, pp 313-346.

Dibbern, J., Winkler, J., and Heinzl, A. "Explaining Variations in Client Extra Costs between Software Projects Offshored to India," *MIS Quarterly* (32:2) 2008, pp 333-366.

Duncan, N.B. "Capturing flexibility of information technology infrastructure: a study of resource characteristics and their measure," *Journal of Management Information Systems* (12:2) 1995, pp 37-57.

Eisenhardt, K.M. "Building Theories from Case Study Research," *Academy of Management Review* (14:4) 1989, pp 532-550.

Eisenhardt, K.M., and Santos, F.M. "Knowledge-Based View: A New Theory of Strategy?," in: *Handbook of Strategy and Management,* A.M. Pettigrew, T. Howard and R. Whittington (eds.), Sage Publications Ltd., London, Thousand Oaks, New Delhi, 2002, pp. 139-164.

Evans, J.S. "Strategic Flexibility for High Technology Manoeuvres: A Conceptual Framework," *Journal of Management Studies* (28:1) 1991, pp 69-89.

Farrell, D. "The Real New Economy," *Harvard Business Review* (81:10) 2003, pp 104-112.

Feurer, R., Chaharbaghi, K., Weber, M., and Wargin, J. "Aligning Strategies, Processes, and IT: A Case Study," *Information Systems Management* (17:1) 2000, pp 23-34.

Foss, N.J. "Edith T. Penrose and the Penrosians - or, why there is still so much to learn from The Theory of the Growth of the Firm," *Economies et Societes* (29) 1999, pp 143-164.

Galunic, D.C., and Rodan, S. "Resource Recombinations in the Firm: Knowledge Structures and the Potential for Schumpeterian Innovation," *Strategic Management Journal* (19:12) 1998, pp 1193-1201.

Gefen, D., and Straub, D.W. "A Practical Guide to Factorial Validity Using PLS-Graph: Tutorial and Annotated Example," *Communications of the Association for Information Systems* (16) 2005, pp 91-109.

Gefen, D., Straub, D.W., and Boudreau, M.-C. "Structural Equation Modeling and Regression: Guidelines for Research Practice," *Communications of the Association for Information Systems* (4:7) 2000, pp 1-77.

Gopal, A., Bostrom, R.P., and Chin, W.W. "Applying Adaptive Structuration Theory to Investigate the Process of Group Support Systems Use," *Journal of Management Information Systems* (9:3) 1993, pp 45-69.

Gordon, J.R., and Gordon, S.R. "Structuring the Interaction between IT and Business Units: Prototypes for Service Delivery," *Information Systems Management* (17:1) 2000, pp 7-16.

Gosain, S., Malhotra, A., and El Sawy, O.A. "Coordinating for Flexibility in e-Business Supply Chains," *Journal of Management Information Systems* (21:3) 2004, pp 7-45.

Grant, R.M. "Prospering in Dynamically-competitive Environments: Organizational Capability as Knowledge Integration," *Organization Science* (7:4) 1996a, pp 375-387.

Grant, R.M. "Toward a knowledge-based theory of the firm," *Strategic Management Journal* (17:10) 1996b, pp 109-122.

Grover, V., Cheon, M.J., and Teng, J.T.C. "The effect of service quality and partnership on the outsourcing of information systems functions," *Journal of Management Information Systems* (12:4) 1996, pp 89-116.

Grover, V., and Segars, A.H. "An empirical evaluation of stages of strategic information systems planning: patterns of process design and effectiveness," *Information & Management* (42:5) 2005, pp 761-779.

Hansen, M.T. "The search-transfer problem: the role of weak ties in sharing knowledge across organization subunits," *Administrative Science Quarterly* (44:1) 1999, pp 82-111.

Henderson, J.C., and Venkatraman, N. "Strategic alignment: Leveraging information technology for transforming organizations," *IBM Systems Journal* (32:1) 1993, pp 3-16.

Hulland, J.S. "Use of Partial Least Squares (PLS) in Strategic Management Research: A Review of four Recent Studies," *Strategic Management Journal* (20:2) 1999, pp 195-204.

Kearns, G.S., and Lederer, A.L. "The effect of strategic alignment on the use of IS-based resources for competitive advantage," *Journal of Strategic Information Systems* (9:4) 2000, pp 265-293.

Kearns, G.S., and Lederer, A.L. "A Resource-Based View of Strategic IT Alignment: How Knowledge Sharing Creates Competitive Advantage," *Decision Sciences* (34:1) 2003, pp 1-29.

Kearns, G.S., and Lederer, A.L. "The impact of industry contextual factors on IT focus and the use of IT for competitive Advantage," *Information & Management* (41:7) 2004, pp 899-919.

Kearns, G.S., and Sabherwal, R. "Strategic Alignment Between Business and Information Technology: A Knowledge-Based View of Behaviors, Outcome, and Consequences," *Journal of Management Information Systems* (23:3) 2006, pp 129-162.

Kettinger, W.J., Lee, C.C., and June "Pragmatic perspectives on the measurement of information systems service quality," in: *MIS Quart*, 1997, pp. 223-240.

Knoll, K., and Jarvenpaa, S.L. "Information technology alignment or "fit" in highly turbulent environments: the concept of flexibility," *Proceedings of the 1994 computer personnel research conference on Reinventing IS: managing information technology in changing organizations: managing information technology in changing organizations*) 1994, pp 1-14.

Kogut, B., and Zander, U. "Knowledge of the Firm, Combinative Capabilities, and the Replication of Technology," *Organization Science* (3:3) 1992, pp 383-397.

Lee, H., Farhoomand, A., and Ho, P. "Innovation Through Supply Chain Reconfiguration," *MIS Quarterly Executive* (3:3) 2004, pp 131-142.

Lee, J.N. "The impact of knowledge sharing, organizational capability and partnership quality on IS outsourcing success," *Information & Management* (38:5) 2001, pp 323-335.

Levina, N., and Ross, J.W. "From the Vendor's Perspective: Exploring the Value Proposition in IT Outsourcing," *MIS Quarterly* (27:3) 2003, pp 331-364.

Liang, H., Saraf, N., Hu, Q., and Xue, Y. "Assimilation of Enterprise Systems: The Effect of Institutional Pressures and the Mediating Role of Top Management," *MIS Quarterly* (31:1) 2007, pp 59-87.

Liebeskind, J.P. "Knowledge, Strategy, and the Theory of the Firm," *Strategic Management Journal* (17:Special Issue: Knowledge and the Firm) 1996, pp 93-107.

Luftman, J., and Kempaiah, R. "An Update on Business-IT Alignment: "A Line" Has Been Drawn," *MIS Quarterly Executive* (6:3) 2007, pp 165-177.

Luftman, J.N. "Assessing IT/Business Alignment," *Information Systems Management* (20:1) 2003, pp 9-15.

Nelson, K.M., and Cooprider, J.G. "The contribution of shared knowledge to IS group performance," *MIS Quarterly* (20:4) 1996, pp 409-432.

Nonaka, I. "A Dynamic Theory of Organizational Knowledge Creation," *Organization Science* (5:1) 1994, pp 14-37.

Nunnally, J.C. *Psychometric theory* McGraw Hill, New York, 1978.

Penrose, E.T. *The theory of the growth of the firm* Wiley, New York, 1959.

Peppard, J., and Ward, J. "Beyond strategic information systems: towards an IS capability," *Journal of Strategic Information Systems* (13:2) 2004, pp 167-194.

Podsakoff, P.M., MacKenzie, S.B., Lee, J.-Y., and Podsakoff, N.P. "Common Method Bias in Behavioral Research: A Critical Review of the Literature and Recommended Remedies," *Journal of Applied Psychology* (88:5) 2003, pp 879-903.

Podsakoff, P.M., and Organ, D.W. "Self-Reports in Organizational Research: Problems and Prospects," *Journal of Management* (12:4) 1986, pp 531-544.

Ravichandran, T., and Lertwongsatien, C. "Effect of Information Systems Resources and Capabilities on Firm Performance: A Resource-Based Perspective," *Journal of Management Information Systems* (21:4) 2005, pp 237-276.

Raymond, L. "Organizational Context and Information Systems Success: A Contingency Approach," *Journal of Management Information Systems* (6:4) 1990, pp 5-20.

Reich, B.H., and Benbasat, I. "Measuring the Linkage Between Business and Information Technology Objectives," *MIS Quarterly* (20:1) 1996, pp 55-81.

Reich, B.H., and Benbasat, I. "Factors that Influence the Social Dimension of Alignment Between Business and Information Technology Objectives," *MIS Quarterly* (24:1) 2000, pp 81-113.

Ringle, C.M., Wende, S., and Will, A. *SmartPLS 2.0 (beta)* University of Hamburg, Hamburg, 2005.

Sambamurthy, V., Bharadwaj, A., and Grover, V. "Shaping Agility through Digital Options: Reconceptualizing the Role of Information Technology in Contemporary Firms," *MIS Quarterly* (27:2) 2003, pp 237-263.

Sambamurthy, V., and Zmud, R.W. "At the Heart of Success: Organizationwide Management Competencies," in: *Steps to the Future: Fresh Thinking on the Management of IT-based Organizational Transformation,* C. Sauer and P. Yetton (eds.), Jossey-Bass Publishers, San Francisco, 1997, pp. 143-163.

Segars, A.H., and Grover, V. "Strategic Information Systems Planning Success: An Investigation of the Construct and Its measurement," *MIS Quarterly* (22:2) 1998, pp 139-163.

Tallon, P.P., and Kraemer, K.L. "Fact or Fiction? A Sensemaking Perspective on the Reality Behind Executives' Perceptions of IT Business Value," *Journal of Management Information Systems* (24:1) 2007, pp 13-54.

Tallon, P.P., Kraemer, K.L., and Gurbaxani, V. "Executives' Perceptions of the Business Value of Information Technology: A Process-Oriented Approach," *Journal of Management Information Systems* (16:4) 2000, pp 145-173.

Teece, D.J. "Explicating Dynamic Capabilities: The Nature and Microfoundations of (Sustainable) Enterprise Performance," *Strategic Management Journal* (28:13) 2007, pp 1319-1350.

Teece, D.J., Pisano, G., and Shuen, A. "Dynamic Capabilities and Strategic Management," *Strategic Management Journal* (18:7) 1997, pp 509-533.

Teo, T.S.H., and Ang, J.S.K. "Critical success factors in the alignment of IS plans with business plans," *International Journal of Information Management* (19:2) 1999, pp 173-185.

Teo, T.S.H., and King, W.R. "Integration between Business Planning and Information Systems Planning: An Evolutionary-Contingency Perspective," *Journal of Management Information Systems* (14:1) 1997, pp 185-214.

Tiwana, A. "Knowledge Partitioning in Outsourced Software Development: A Field Study," International Conference on Information Systems (ICIS), Seattle, Washington, 2003.

Tiwana, A. "Beyond the Black Box: Knowledge Overlaps in Software Outsourcing," *IEEE Software* (21:5) 2004, pp 51-58.

Tiwana, A., Bharadwaj, A., and Sambamurthy, V. "The Antecedents of Information Systems Development Capability in Firms: A Knowledge Integration Perspective," Proceedings of the Twenty-Fourth International Conference in Information Systems, Seattle, Washington, USA, 2003, pp. 246-258.

Wagner, H.-T. *A Resource-based Perspective on IT Business Alignment and Firm Performance: Theoretical foundation and empirical evidence* ibidem-Verlag, Stuttgart, 2007.

Weill, P., Subramani, M., and Broadbent, M. "Building IT Infrastructure for Strategic Agility," *MIT Sloan Management Review* (44:1) 2002, pp 57-65.

Worren, N., Moore, K., and Cardona, P. "Modularity, Strategic Flexibility, and Firm Performance: A Study of the Home Appliance Industry," *Strategic Management Journal* (23:12) 2002, pp 1123-1140.

Young-Ybarra, C., and Wiersema, M. "Strategic Flexibility in Information Technology Alliances: The Influence of Transaction Cost Economics and Social Exchange Theory," *Organization Science* (10:4) 1999, pp 439-459.

Zhu, K., and Kraemer, K.L. "e-Commerce Metrics for Net-Enhanced Organizations: Assessing the Value of e-Commerce to Firm Performance in the Manufacturing Sector," *Information Systems Research* (13:3) 2002, pp 275-295.

10 Appendix

	Group With Low Levels of Documentation				Group With High Levels of Documentation			
	AVE	Composite Reliability	R Square	Cronbach's Alpha	AVE	Composite Reliability	R Square	Cronbach's Alpha
Cognition	.574	.799	.410	.641	.614	.827	.559	.688
Communication	.855	.946		.916	.892	.961		.940
IT Provider Flexibility	.631	.895	.450	.854	.600	.882	.342	.835
Shared Knowledge	.658	.850	.000	.726	.574	.798	.059	.717

Table 9: Comparison of Quality Criteria for the Two Sub-Samples

	Group With Low Levels of Documentation				Group With High Levels of Documentation			
	Cognition	Communication	IT Provider Flexibility	Shared Knowledge	Cognition	Communication	IT Provider Flexibility	Shared Knowledge
Cognition	.760				.785			
Communication	.208	.910			.363	.944		
IT Provider Flexibility	.554	.072	.794		.724	.234	.775	
Shared Knowledge	.580	.069	.694	.806	.457	.229	.577	.751

Table 10: Correlations of Latent Variables and AVE Square Root (Shaded Cells) in the Two Sub-Samples

The Impact of Alignment on Outsourcing Outcomes: Empirical Evidence from the German Banking Industry

Sebastian F. Martin
E-Finance Lab
Institute for Information Systems
Goethe University, Frankfurt, Germany
smartin@wiwi.uni-frankfurt.de

Abstract

Drawing on a sample of 153 application management outsourcing relationships from the German banking industry, this paper analyzes the impact of client's internal IT-business alignment on the relationship quality between client and provider and on the provider's service quality. We find that clients who exhibit higher levels of firm-internal IT-business alignment are more likely to experience a better relationship quality with, and receive a better service quality from, the IT provider. Moreover, we find that time has a mitigating effect on this relationship such that the impact of client-internal IT-business alignment on the outcomes of outsourcing is stronger in young relationships than it is in older relationships.

1 Introduction

Despite the considerable growth that IT outsourcing (ITO) has seen during the past decade, there are still relatively few organizations reporting success, especially in the incipient period of the outsourcing arrangement. Clients engage into ITO relationships seeking to gain advantages like specialization, cost savings in service provision, and flexibility, but are often disappointed by the experienced outcomes. Prior literature has acknowledged that establishing and maintaining a positive client-provider relationship is key to achieving outsourcing success (Lee et al. 1999). While attempts have been made to identify and categorize the different drivers and dimensions of relationship quality (Blumenberg 2008; Goles et al. 2005; Lee et al. 1999), little is known so far about the influence of the client's *internal* organizational context on its relationship with the vendor and on the outcomes of outsourcing. This perspective has only scarcely been tackled so far, although there is indication in the literature that, from the client's point of view, aligning internal goals and processes with external arrangements is crucial for achieving outsourcing benefits. For example, Ranganathan and Balaji (2007) report that firms need to carefully evaluate their own *organizational readiness* for outsourcing (which they define as the firm's ability to prepare its internal organization to undertake outsourcing activities), before engaging into outsourcing relationships. Alborz et al. (2004) found that alignment between the outsourcing project and the client's overall strategy was an important impact factor for the quality of the outsourcing relationship because if the client's outsourcing objectives are not aligned with its business objectives, the service offered by the provider may not satisfy the user needs and requirements.

Especially in their incipient phase, outsourcing relationships require extensive knowledge exchange between client and provider, because the provider needs to acquire a thorough understanding of its client's specifics in terms of business processes and IT infrastructure (Dibbern et al. 2008). Thus, while on the IT provider side there is the need to build up the absorptive capacity that allows for acquiring and integrating client-related knowledge, (Dibbern et al. 2008; Lee 2001), it is the *client's* responsibility to internally coordinate the aggregation of firm-specific knowledge among different stakeholders within the organization and to make it available to the IT provider.

How can clients prepare their internal organizations to foster outsourcing success? In an earlier article (Martin et al. 2008), we studied the impact of internal business process documentation, as a means for inter-organizational knowledge sharing, on the link between IT business alignment and IT provider flexibility in outsourcing relationships. We could empirically demonstrate that having up-to-date process documentation enhanced the client's outsourcing readiness by fostering knowledge transferability. In this paper, we follow this path one step further, asking whether *intra*-organizational *alignment* between the client firm's IT and business domains may affect the *inter*-organizational *relationship* between the client and the outsourcing vendor. Our main proposition in this paper is that thorough intra-organizational alignment at the operational level enhances the client's preparedness for successful outsourcing by enabling the client to deliver required information about its own business processes and systems to the IT provider more accurately and reliably, which ultimately translates into higher service quality. However, we find this inter-organizational impact of client-internal alignment to be contingent upon the age of the ongoing relationship, such that client-internal alignment affects the quality of service provision more strongly in younger relationships.

We test our hypotheses by performing a quantitative analysis on a dataset obtained from a survey carried out in 2008 among Germany's largest 1,000 banks, focusing on *application management outsourcing*[1] relationships between banks and IT service providers.

2 Research Background

2.1 IT Business Alignment

IT business alignment (ITBA) has been one of the main concerns of IT executives for many years (Luftman et al. 2004) and the importance of ITBA as one of the primary means for delivering IT business value has been stressed out repeatedly (Chan et al. 2007; Reich et al. 2000; Tiwana et al. 2003). Prior

---

[1] Following Levina and Ross (2003), we refer to application management outsourcing as the ongoing maintenance, support, and enhancement of an outsourced application by an IT provider.

research has distinguished between intellectual and social dimensions of alignment (Reich et al. 2000). While the intellectual dimension reflects the match between IT and business strategies, concepts, and plans, the social dimension of alignment reflects the bonds between IT and business executives, like communication and shared domain knowledge (Reich et al. 2000). Tiwana et al. (2003) and Tan and Galupe (2006) added a cognitive perspective on the linkages between executives from IT and business domains. Tiwana (2003) found that cognitive linkages between IT and business executives directly and positively influenced knowledge integration. Tan and Galupe (2006) found indication that a higher level of cognitive commonality between business and IT executives was positively related to higher levels of alignment. These conceptualizations of alignment as cognitive relationships between executives from the two domains have strong parallels with the social dimension of alignment (Chan et al. 2007).

Although literature acknowledges that "alignment should be present at all levels of the organization" (Chan et al. 2007), most alignment research has focused on alignment at the *strategic level* between IT and business *executives* (Bergeron et al. 2004). However, investigating alignment at the *operational* level is important, because "strategies are only effective when they are translated into actions readily" (Feurer et al. 2000, p.23), meaning that strategies need to be transformed into "daily business" (Gordon et al. 2000).

Integrating Reich and Benbasat's (2000) insights about the social dimension of alignment with the concept of cognitive IS-business linkages (Tiwana et al. 2003), Beimborn, Wagner, and colleagues (Beimborn et al. 2006; Wagner 2007) bring strategic alignment down to an operational level, developing a construct of operational ITBA which consists of three dimensions: communication, shared domain knowledge, and cognitive linkages between employees from the IT and business domains at *mid-management and operative levels*. In their conceptualization, *communication* refers to the kind and quality of the interaction patterns between business and IT people. *Shared domain knowledge* refers to both, IT-knowledgeable business people as well as business-knowledgeable IT people. Finally, the *cognitive dimension* refers to shared mutual understanding of common goals, mutual respect, and trust between IS and business people. For the purpose of our research, we adopt this view of operational ITBA and use this concept in our research model.

2.2 A Knowledge-based Perspective on Outsourcing Relationships

Recent literature has increasingly investigated IT outsourcing relationships from a knowledge-based perspective (e.g., Currie 2003; Dibbern et al. 2008; Tiwana 2003). Originating from the resource-based view (Penrose 1959), the knowledge-based theory (KBT) (Grant 1996) views knowledge as the most important resource of the firm and regards knowledge integration, spanning a broad range of knowledge domains, to be the main mechanism for achieving and sustaining competitive advantage (Kogut et al. 1992). Scholars argue that "knowledge is arguably the most important asset that firms possess – a key source of both Ricardian and monopoly rents" (Liebeskind 1996, p.93).

Knowledge *asymmetries* between client and provider are characteristic for outsourcing relationships, because each organization disposes of a unique set of human resources and therefore of a unique repository of knowledge (Dibbern et al. 2008). Thus, knowledge needs to be constantly shared between the client and the provider because "the client continually produces new application domain knowledge which reflects its constantly changing business requirements" (Dibbern et al. 2008, p.337), while the vendor needs to understand "the wants, needs, constraints, and behaviors of the customers" Goles (2003, p.201). For example, if the outsourcing provider is required to perform maintenance and enhancement operations to the application that supports one of its client's business processes, it needs to acquire knowledge not just about the application itself, but also about the associated business process as well as about the application's interfaces to adjacent information systems.

Simonin (Simonin 1999, p.597) notes that "knowledge transfer depends on how easily that knowledge can be transported, interpreted, and absorbed" and empirically demonstrates that the transferability of knowledge is negatively influenced by its characteristics such as tacitness, complexity, specificity, and ambiguity. Thus, on the one hand, prior literature has pointed out that the provider needs the absorptive capacity which allows him to acquire and integrate client-related knowledge (Dibbern et al. 2008; Lee 2001). Mastering this "challenge of understanding the client's unique business processes and infrastructure" (Dibbern et al. 2008, p.340) is important because missing knowledge about the client's specifics can result in low service quality and delays. This is, however, only "one side of the coin". *On the other hand*, namely, the provider can only acquire client-specific knowledge if this knowledge is *made available* to him by the client. For that matter, the client is confronted with the need to internally coordinate different stakeholders from business and IT domains in order to aggregate complex and idiosyncratic knowledge, to eliminate ambiguity and to make the necessary information available to the IT provider. To our knowledge, this perspective has not been tackled by prior research, leaving a gap worth being investigated more deeply.

3 Research Model and Hypotheses

This paper argues that in outsourcing relationships, the quality of communication between people from the different inner-organizational domains of the client firm has an impact on the firm's relationship with the vendor and on the quality of the service provided by the vendor. Figure 1 depicts this association. The left side of the model (Hypotheses 1 to 4) describes causal links between the different dimensions of operational IT business alignment grounded within the client's own organizational context. Hypotheses 5 to 7 describe the impact of these constructs on the quality of the inter-organizational relationship and on the provided service quality. The last two hypotheses (H8 and H9) posit that the inter-organizational effect of the client firm's internal alignment is contingent upon the *age* of its ongoing relationship to the outsourcing vendor. More precisely, these hypotheses posit that the inter-organizational impact of client-internal alignment becomes *weaker*, the older and more well-established the outsourcing relationship is.

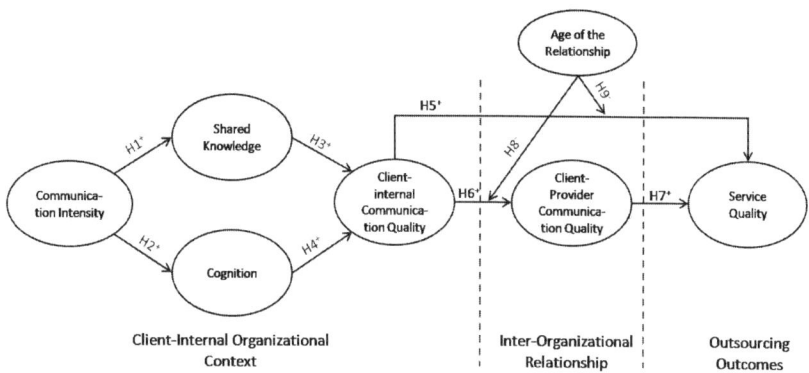

Figure 1: Research Model

3.1 Intra-organizational IT-Business Alignment and Communication Quality

Chan and Reich observe that "the importance of regular communication between IT and business people cannot be overemphasized" (Chan et al. 2007, p.311). Frequent information exchange enhances the transfer of knowledge, facilitating knowledge sharing (Alavi et al. 2001) and leading to tight cognitive linkages between the members of the two domains (Tiwana et al. 2003). At the strategic level of the firm, this assertion is backed by the findings of Athanassiou and Neigh (2000), who found a positive effect of face-to-face communications on the development and maintenance of tacit knowledge for top managers. Moreover, Lind and Zmud (1991) empirically found that frequent communication was associated with a convergence in mutual understanding between managers from IT and business domains. This reasoning should hold true for lower organizational levels, as well. Thus, our first two hypotheses are:

H1: Higher levels of communication intensity are associated with higher levels of shared domain knowledge between the employees from clients' IT and business domains.

H2: Higher levels of communication intensity are associated with higher levels of cognitive linkages between the employees from clients' IT and business domains.

Nelson and Cooprider (1996) and Reich and Benbasat (1996; 2000) developed the notion of shared domain knowledge which refers to the personal knowledge of IT and business people about each other's domain (see also Bassellier 2001; Bassellier et al. 2003). KBT posits that a certain amount of common knowledge between individuals with different specialized knowledge – as it is the case with IT and business employees – is important because it permits individuals to "integrate aspects of knowledge which are not common between them. [...] if the individuals have entirely separate knowledge bases, then integration cannot occur beyond the most primitive level" (Grant 1996, pp.115-116). Thus, higher levels of common knowledge enable business and IT people to effectively exchange and integrate accurate and reliable information, which translates into higher communication quality between business and IT domains. This assertion is supported by Kearns and Sabherwal (2007, p.133), who note that "successful knowledge integration requires that the concerned individuals possess an underlying base of shared domain knowledge". We thus hypothesize:

H3: Higher levels of shared domain knowledge between members of client's IT and business domains are associated with higher levels of intra-organizational communication quality.

Our next hypothesis pertains to cognitive linkages between business and IT people as enablers for effective communication. Tiwana et al. (2003) found strong support for the positive influence of cognitive linkages on knowledge integration in information systems development projects. They note that "business units that share a vision with the IT unit are more likely to share and exchange their resources because they are better able to envision the potential value of their recombination" (Tiwana et al. 2003, p.249). Thus, strong cognitive linkages enable the aggregation of accurate and reliable information across the client's business and IT domains. Moreover, strong cognitive linkages between business and IT side enable individuals from one domain to serve as receptors for the other domain – to sense and communicate information that the other side otherwise might not get or might not be able to interpret, thus facilitating effective knowledge integration (Ross et al. 1996; Tiwana et al. 2003; Wagner 2007). Therefore, we formulate:

H4: Higher levels of cognitive linkages between members of client's IT and business domains are associated with higher levels of intra-organizational communication quality.

3.2 IT Outsourcing Relationship and Service Quality

IT outsourcing relationships have been characterized as complex and knowledge-intensive relationships, which require the integration of knowledge from different pools within as well as across organizations (Martin et al. 2008; Tiwana 2003). Lee (2001) empirically demonstrated that knowledge sharing between client and provider was a major predictor for outsourcing success. Effective knowledge sharing is reflected by the accuracy and reliability of the information exchange. Lee et al. (1999) found empirical support for the positive relationship between inter-organizational communication quality and partnership quality between client and vendor. Our main argument in this paper is that in such outsourcing relationships, the quality of client-internal IT business alignment has repercussions on the quality of the communication between client and provider as well as on the quality of the service provided by the outsourcing vendor. The idea hereby is that internally well-aligned organizations are better able to integrate complex organizational information and to communicate this information to their external partners with precision and accuracy, which has a positive influence on the provider's service quality.

Outsourcing relationships in which an IT application is maintained and enhanced by an external provider typically entail many smaller or larger projects aimed at performing changes to that particular application. For example, the business domain may request certain functional improvements to that application or the business process supported by the application might change, in which case the system needs to be adapted to support the altered workflow. If a particular change is needed, the client usually formulates the requirements in a so-called change request. The speed and accuracy with which the provider reacts to such requests, implementing the required changes, partly depends on the accuracy of the client's indications. Changes may quickly become costly if the client fails to formulate change requests precisely and detailed enough, because inaccurate change requests increase the amount of effort that the provider needs to undertake in order to fulfill them correctly. This translates into delays and possibly implementation failures. For the client firm, this means that proper coordination across the internal business and IT domains needs to take place, because a desired change has to be described such that it reflects the functional needs of the client firm's business domain as well as the technical requirements and restrictions of its IT domain. This leads us to the following hypothesis:

H5: Higher levels of client-internal communication quality between members of the client's business and IT domains are associated with higher levels of service quality of the provider.

Communication quality has been repeatedly deemed a key factor for the success of inter-organizational partnerships. Timely, accurate, and relevant information exchange is essential for achieving the goals in a partnership (Mao et al. 2008; Mohr et al. 1994) while limiting communication and information exchange may inhibit the learning which is necessary for the IT vendor to provide the agreed service (Norman 2004). As argued earlier in this paper, the service provider needs to learn about the client firm's particularities in terms of business processes associated with the outsourced application as well as adjacent information systems that might be affected by changes to the outsourced application (Dibbern et al. 2008; Lee 2001). Thus, especially in younger relationships, successful outsourcing requires a massive transfer of knowledge between client and provider because much of the application domain knowledge held by the client needs to be acquired by the provider (Martin et al. 2008). "This would include the transfer of knowledge about the business processes and the user information needs that are to be reflected by the software application" (Dibbern et al. 2008, p.337).

Hence, besides its dependency upon precisely formulated change requests, the vendor's service quality is also dependent on the quality of the general information with regard to client's business processes and technical conditions. Conversely, the client needs to be able to aggregate firm-internal knowledge and make it explicit – for example in the form of precise and reliable technical and process documentation – in order to provide the required information to the outsourcing vendor. We argue that a higher inner-organizational communication quality within the client's own firm enables a more effective and reliable transfer of client-related knowledge to the vendor. This higher inter-organizational communication quality in turn enhances the vendor's overall ability to provide prompt and reliable services. We thus formulate:

H6: Higher levels of client-internal communication quality are associated with higher levels of client-provider communication quality.

H7: Higher levels of client-provider communication quality are associated with higher levels of service quality.

3.3 The Mitigating Effect of Time

We noted in the preceding sections that the postulated relationships between client's inner-organizational communication quality and the outcomes of outsourcing were especially salient in young relationships. Indeed, as the relationship grows more mature, the provider has the time and opportunity to develop a deeper knowledge about its client's particularities in terms of business processes and technical conditions. This reduces the impact of the client's inner-organizational settings on the quality of the inter-organizational relationship and of the provided service. In a mature relationship, when asking the provider to perform a certain change to the outsourced application, the client may not need to communicate information about the related business process at the same level of detail as it would need to do in a young relationship. Deeper knowledge about the client's particularities enables the IT provider to correctly interpret even requests which are formulated more rudimentarily and still respond quickly and reliably to the request. Similarly, the quality of the general communication between client and provider is less dependent on the client's inner-organizational alignment once the relevant processes and technical conditions have been documented and this knowledge has been transferred to the provider. These assertions lead us to following hypotheses:

H8: Time mitigates the impact of client-internal communication quality on client-provider communication quality such that the impact of client-internal communication quality on client-provider communication quality is stronger in younger outsourcing relationships than it is in older relationships.

H9: Time mitigates the impact of client-internal communication quality on provider's service quality such that the impact of client-internal communication quality on provider's service quality is stronger in younger outsourcing relationships than it is in older relationships.

4 Methodology

4.1 Data Collection

Data for testing the hypothesized model was collected using a field survey with Germany's largest 1,000 banks. We chose this particular sector because business processes in banks are especially IT-intensive, since IT represents the only production resource besides people. Moreover, due to the particular structure of this industry – more than 80% of all German banks are public savings banks or credit cooperatives – banks have usually outsourced large parts of their IT to joint data processing centers. This is why we could be confident that the banks addressed by us had really outsourced the application we were referring to in our questionnaire to an IT provider, while the sample also allowed for homogeneity in variables uncontrolled for.

Prior to sending out the questionnaire, we identified for each bank in the sample the manager who was responsible for the relationship with the vendor firm which provided management services for a particular application, namely, the application that supports the process of granting and managing mortgage loans. Depending on the size of the bank, this person was usually a mid-level manager (the so-called vendor manager). This is consistent with our focus on the operational level of the firm, as opposed to the strategic level. Moreover, focusing on a particular application allowed us to create comparable settings and to control for unwanted side effects. We personally addressed the questionnaire to that person. As a result, we achieved an effective response rate of 16.0% (160 returned questionnaires). A number of 153 questionnaires showed no missing values and were used for analysis.

4.2 Measure Development

We derived the questionnaire items from recent scientific literature and extensively validated them in pre-tests and expert workshops prior to the survey in order to minimize semantic bias.

Operational IT-business alignment within the client's organization was measured based on the constructs developed by Beimborn, Wagner, and colleagues (Beimborn et al. 2007; Wagner 2007). In their conceptualization, *communication* refers to the "kind and quality of the interaction patterns" (Wagner 2007) between business and IT domains of an organization. Since this definition entails both quantitative as well as qualitative aspects, we further refine this dimension, explicitly distinguishing between quantitative and qualitative aspects. Therefore, we refer to client-internal *communication intensity* as the frequency and amount of information exchanged while client-internal *communication quality* captures the effectiveness and reliability of the information exchange between IT and business people. *Shared domain knowledge* is a form of tacit knowledge which refers to both "IT-knowledgeable business managers and business-knowledgeable IT managers" (Reich et al. 2000, p.84). For the purpose of this study, we adopt a bilateral view of shared knowledge and explicitly distinguish between *IT knowledge of business employees* and *business knowledge of IT employees* (Bassellier 2001; Bassellier et al. 2004). Finally, *cognitive linkages* – elements which form the critical foundation of a good relationship between IT and business people – were captured by measuring the extent of mutual respect and trust between employees from the two domains (Martin et al. 2008; Tiwana et al. 2003).

Inter-organizational *client-provider communication quality, which* is a key indicator for the quality of client-vendor relationships (Blumenberg et al. 2008; Lee et al. 1999; Mao et al. 2008), was captured by measuring the effectiveness and reliability of the information exchanged between the two organizations (Mohr et al. 1994).

Service quality was measured along two dimensions based on the SERVQUAL instrument (Parasuraman et al. 1988): responsiveness – reflecting the vendor's willingness to help its client and provide prompt service – and reliability – reflecting the vendor's ability to perform the service dependably and accurately (Kettinger et al. 1997). The indicators used to assess each construct are depicted in Table 1.

The Impact of Alignment on Outsourcing Outcomes

Construct (scale)	Dimension	Item	Indicator
Client's Inner-Organizational Context: Operational IT-Business Alignment (5point Likert)	Communication intensity	CINT1	There are meetings on a regular basis between IT unit and business unit.
		CINT2	The business unit is actively involved in IT planning.
	Cognition	COG1	There exists a lot of mutual trust between IT unit and business unit.
		COG2	There exists a lot of mutual respect between IT unit and business unit.
		COG3	The business unit sees our IT as an important consultant.
	IT Knowledge of Business Employees	ITKN1	The employees of the business unit have strong knowledge about IT projects.
		ITKN2	The employees of the business unit have enough IT skills to understand the time needed for changes.
	Business Knowledge of IT Employees	BUKN1	The employees of the IT unit know the credit process.
		BUKN2	The employees of the IT unit are able to interpret business-related problems and to develop solutions.
		BUKN3	Our IT staff has sufficient banking know how to understand business problems and come up with solutions.
Inter-Organizational Relationship: Communication Quality (7point Likert)	Client-internal Communication Quality	CICQ1	Communication between IT unit and business unit in our bank is very good.
		CICQ2	IT unit and business unit effectively exchange information.
	Client-Provider Communication Quality	CPCQ1	Both parties in the outsourcing relationship communicate well with each other.
		CPCQ2	We effectively exchange information with the outsourcing provider.
		CPCQ3	Our provider's reports are clear and comprehensible.
Outsourcing Outcomes: Service Quality (5point Likert)	Responsiveness	RES1	The service provider reacts fast if there are problems.
		RES2	The service provider shows good readiness to respond to our requests.
		RES3	Provider staff deals with us in a caring fashion.
	Reliability	REL1	The provider solves problems reliably.
		REL2	Applications and services are provided as promised.
		REL3	There are never any critical system failures.

Table 1: Construct Specification (Original questionnaire was provided in German)

5   Analysis and Results

5.1   PLS Measurement Model

The statistical analysis was conducted using the Partial Least Square (PLS) approach, employing SmartPLS 2.0 (Ringle et al. 2005). PLS was chosen for two reasons. First, PLS is more appropriate if theory is untested in an application domain or tentative (Gopal et al. 1993), and second, our data set predominantly consists of not normally distributed variables, which prevents the use of covariance-based instruments. For testing the model, we used only reflective measures.

Factor	Item	CINT	BUKN	ITKN	COG	CICQ	CPCQ	REL	RES
Communication Intensity (CINT)	CINT1	.849	.295	.330	.327	.584	.131	.147	.244
	CINT2	.891	.336	.333	.438	.448	.198	.038	.224
Business Knowledge IT Employees (BUKN)	BUKN1	.397	.918	.200	.304	.324	.204	.062	.222
	BUKN2	.338	.927	.223	.318	.343	.222	.196	.280
	BUKN3	.193	.828	.223	.268	.237	.214	.187	.291
IT Knowledge Business Employees (ITKN)	ITKN1	.322	.181	.916	.397	.369	.123	.170	.294
	ITKN2	.376	.254	.922	.274	.343	.191	.104	.287
Cognition (COG)	COG1	.372	.223	.304	.895	.597	.100	.064	.139
	COG2	.310	.330	.266	.881	.575	.091	.040	.128
	COG3	.467	.323	.374	.840	.547	.154	.093	.215
Client-Internal Communication Quality (CICQ)	CICQ1	.587	.362	.346	.552	.916	.173	.196	.173
	CICQ2	.461	.252	.352	.640	.886	.186	.002	.131
Client-Provider Communication Quality (CPCQ)	CPCQ1	.128	.222	.191	.080	.115	.901	.408	.561
	CPCQ2	.192	.136	.121	.146	.168	.874	.242	.480
	CPCQ3	.189	.253	.135	.132	.240	.861	.374	.472
Reliability (REL)	REL1	.050	.110	.110	.042	.024	.423	.824	.627
	REL2	.099	.143	.155	.074	.118	.262	.772	.413
	REL3	.097	.122	.091	.070	.148	.241	.781	.362
Responsiveness (RES)	RES1	.127	.132	.204	.150	.126	.498	.521	.831
	RES2	.314	.311	.340	.120	.179	.410	.421	.811
	RES3	.212	.262	.222	.181	.107	.483	.505	.777

Table 2: Item-Factor Loadings and Cross Loadings for Full Sample

Content validity was assured by deriving indicator questions from prior research and by using pre-tests to eliminate ambiguities. The insights from the pre-tests were used to adapt some of the indicator questions to the intended meaning. Each one of the constructs exhibited the required indicator reliability, convergent validity, and discriminant validity (see Tables 2, 3 and 4).

Factor	CINT	BUKN	ITKN	COG	CICQ	CPCQ	REL	RES
CINT	.901							
BUKN	.364	.892						
ITKN	.380	.238	.919					
COG	.444	.334	.364	.872				
CICQ	.586	.345	.387	.657	.901			
CPCQ	.192	.237	.172	.134	.199	.879		
REL	.102	.157	.148	.077	.117	.396	.793	
RES	.268	.289	.316	.186	.170	.575	.599	.806

Table 3: Correlation Matrix and AVE Square Roots (shaded cells) for Full Sample

Factor	Composite Reliability	AVE	Cronbach's Alpha	R Square
CINT	.862	.758	.682	--
BUKN	.921	.796	.874	.132
ITKN	.916	.845	.816	.145
COG	.905	.761	.843	.197
CICQ	.896	.812	.770	.470
CPCQ	.911	.773	.853	.039
REL	.835	.628	.705	.158
RES	.848	.650	.731	.334

Table 4: Quality Measures for Latent Variables for Full Sample

5.2 Non-Response Bias and Common Method Bias

To test for non-response bias, we distinguished between early respondents and late respondents (managers who responded after a reminder (Worren et al. 2002)). We conducted T-tests for comparing the group means for all indicators as well as for all latent variable scores. Following Kearns and Lederer (2004), we treated the late respondents (51.9% of all respondents) as non-respondents, because they share similarities with non-respondents. There were no significant differences between the two groups. This indicates that non-response bias cannot be assumed.

Common method bias may occur when a single source is being used for assessing both the independent as well as the dependent constructs. Podsakoff et al. (2003) distinguish between procedural and statistical remedies to cope with common method bias. The procedural remedies refer to measures carried out before data collection and are related to the design of the questionnaire. The statistical remedies are tests after data collection. To address procedural remedies, we removed ambiguous and complex items from the questionnaire by using pre-tests; reverse-coded items were grouped and used to counter acquiescence effects, and anonymity of respondents was assured to counter social desirability effects. We used two methods to address statistical remedies. First, we followed the approach suggested by Podsakoff et al. (2003) and described by Liang et al. (2007): we converted all indicators into single-indicator constructs and allowed them to load both on their own substantive construct as well as on a latent common method factor in order to verify that the common method factor does not provide a substantial explanation of the variance compared to the original latent variable. We found no significant influence of the common method factor on any of the single-indicator constructs, which on the other hand were all significantly explained by their own substantive construct at $p<0.01$. This result is indicative for the absence of a common method bias in our data.

Second, we included a 'marker variable' in the questionnaire – i.e., a construct which is theoretically independent of the research model underlying our study (Lindell et al. 2001). This marker variable showed no significant correlation with any of the indicators of our research model which again suggests that common method bias needs not to be assumed.

5.3 Test of Hypotheses

While the hypothesized links between the constructs of our model (H1-7) were tested on the full sample of 153 responses, the mitigating effect of time (H8, H9) was tested by conducting a multi-group comparison. We chose to conduct a multi-group comparison rather than moderation tests because the discriminant variable "age of the relationship" was surveyed not on a purely metric scale but also "categorial", since respondents could choose whether to indicate the exact year when the provider took over the credit processing system (in case this information was available to them) or to mark whether the relationship was older than ten years. From the total of 153 returned questionnaires with no missing values, 74 respondents indicated the exact year of the outsourcing (11 of them stating an age of the relationship which was older than 10 years), 67 respondents just marked the checkbox "older than ten years", and 12 respondents marked the checkbox "don't know" and therefore had to be excluded from the grouping.

In a first step, we divided the sample into two groups of banks with relationships of 5 years or less (46 respondents) vs. older than 5 years (95 respondents). In a second step, we set the grouping break point at 10 years, obtaining groups with 63 respondents (10 years or less) vs. 78 respondents (with relationships older than 10 years). In both steps, we performed 2,000 bootstraps of the PLS model with each sub-sample. The multi-group comparisons were done by a T-test on the resulting distribution of path coefficients.

We evaluated the measurement models for both groups of sub-samples (groups with break point set at five years and groups with break point set at 10 years) and found configural invariance in both groups of sub-samples. The corresponding descriptive statistics and reliabilities are reported in Tables 6 to 9 in the Appendix.

The test results of hypotheses 1 to 7 on the overall sample of 153 responses are depicted in Figure 2, while the results of the multi-group comparison are depicted in Table 5. In the overall sample, we could only find weak support for the hypothesized effect of client-internal communication quality on client-provider communication quality (H6) and no support at all for the effect of client-internal communication quality on service quality (H5a, H5b). However, this picture changed considerably when we included the age of the relationship as a mitigating variable into our analysis (H8, H9). After setting the grouping break point at 5 years, the link between client-internal communication quality and client-provider communication quality became highly significant with a strong path coefficient of .490 in the group with relationships aged 5 years or less, while it showed no significance in the group with relationships older than 5 years. After setting the grouping break point at 10 years, we found a slight decline of the path coefficient in the group with relationships aged 10 years or less, as compared to the group with 5 years or less, which again is indicative of the mitigating effect of time on this relationship.

We get a similar picture when analyzing the hypothesized mitigating effect of time on the relationship between client-internal communication quality and service quality (with the two dimensions reliability – H9a, and responsiveness – H9b). The hypothesized effects are weakly significant in the group with relationships of 5 years or less and the values decline when setting the grouping break point at 10 years. This again indicates that, in time, the provider's service quality becomes less dependent on the client's ability to align internally and communicate effectively.

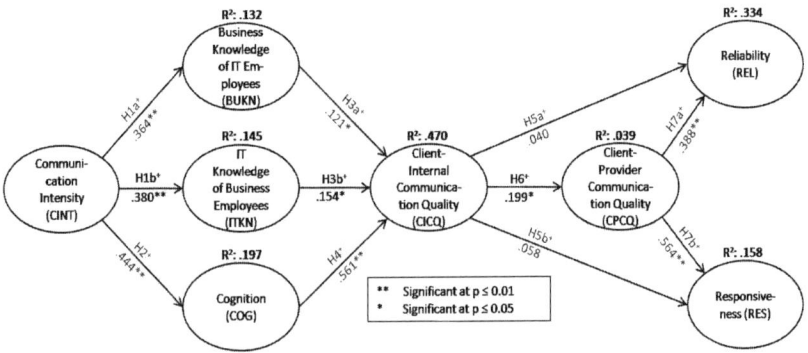

Figure 2: PLS Results – Complete Sample (N = 153; Test of H1-7)

	Original path coefficient		Average path coefficient from 2000 bootstraps (st. dev)		T-test on pair-wise difference between groups ≠ 0
Grouping Break Point: 5 Years	Group with relationship age ≤ 5 years (n = 46)	Group with relationship age > 5 years (n = 95)	Group with relationship age ≤ 5 years (n = 46)	Group with relationship age > 5 years (n = 95)	(T, p)
H8: Effect of relationship age on the link CICQ → CPCQ	.490**	.131	.506 (.096)	.121 (.153)	(94.627, .000)
H9a: Effect of relationship age on the link CICQ → REL	.305*	-.133	.333 (.174)	-.067 (.174)	(72.083, .000)
H9b: Effect of relationship age on the link CICQ → RES	.255*	-.050	.266 (.136)	-.052 (.094)	(86.565, .000)
Grouping Break Point: 10 Years	Group with relationship age <= 10 years (n = 63)	Group with relationship age > 10 years (n = 78)	Group with relationship age <= 10 years (n = 63)	Group with relationship age > 10 years (n = 78)	(T, p)
H8: Effect of relationship age on the link CICQ → CPCQ	.400**	.103	.410 (.095)	.097 (.177)	(68.573, .000)
H9a: Effect of relationship age on the link CICQ → REL	.287*	-.207	.310 (.132)	-.127 (.220)	(75.353, .000)
H9b: Effect of relationship age on the link CICQ → RES	.147	-.045	.159 (.114)	-.047 (.107)	(58.101, .000)

Legend: CICQ: Client-Internal Communication Quality; CPCQ: Client-Provider Communication Quality; REL: Reliability; RES: Responsiveness; ** significant at p<.01; * significant at p<.05

Table 5: Multi-Group Comparison of Path Coefficients (Test of H8 and H9)

With regard to the client-internal organizational context, our hypotheses pertaining to the relationships between the different dimensions of operational alignment were all strongly supported, with the exception of H3, which in both cases (the effect of business knowledge of IT employees – H3a – and of IT knowledge of business employees – H3b – on client-internal communication quality) were only weakly supported.

6 Discussion and Limitations

The results of this study show that client-internal IT business alignment at an operational level has significant inter-organizational repercussions. We found strong empirical evidence for the considerable impact of client-internal communication quality on the quality of inter-organizational communication between the client and the outsourcing vendor, which in turn has a strong positive impact on vendor's service quality. We also found empirical support for the hypothesized direct effect of client-internal communication quality on vendor's reliability and responsiveness. Thus, thorough inner-organizational alignment allows the client firm to internally aggregate knowledge and make qualitative general information about the own business processes and technological conditions available to the vendor, and it also allows the client to formulate complete and precise change requests which leave no room for potentially costly ambiguities.

However, the multi-group comparison clearly shows that this boundary-spanning effect of the client's inner-organizational context is contingent upon the age of the client-vendor relationship. In settled relationships, well-versed communication structures as well as learning effects allow the provider to keep up effective communication with the client and to provide a steady service quality even if the client's internal resources are less aligned.

With regard to the client's inner-organizational context, an interesting finding is that cognitive linkages between employees from the business and IT domains have by far the strongest impact on client-internal communication quality. Not only is this link highly significant, but the strength of the path coefficient (.560) is considerable. Thus, cognitive linkages between IT and business people prove to be indispensable for the exchange of accurate and reliable information.

Our approach involves some limitations. First, we used IT managers' perceptions as a proxy for internal alignment as well as interorganizational communication quality and service quality. This of course represents only the client's view of the story. In addition, while managers' perceptions of the service quality may be based on objective measures, the assessment of inter-organizational communication quality is rather subjective – as perceived by that person. However, the use of perceptions is widely accepted in IS research (Bergeron et al. 2004; Chan et al. 1997; Cragg et al. 2002), because there is evidence in literature that they correlate with objective measures. "Perceptions may therefore not be entirely accurate, but, in the subconscious reasoning of executives who are trying to give a reasoned response [...] it is accurate enough" (Tallon et al. 2007, p.19). Another limitation is the threat of bias stemming from the single-person and single-point-in-time measurement as well as from the focus on only one industry and only one country, which may prevent generalizability. However, this narrow focus may also be seen as strength of our study, because it excludes much of the potential side-effects from uncontrolled variables that might occur in a wider frameset (Chiasson et al. 2005).

7 Theoretical Contribution and Practical Implications

This paper is among the first to consider the impact of client's inner-organizational context on the inter-organizational relationship with the outsourcing vendor and on the outcomes of outsourcing. We could demonstrate that effective knowledge transfer depends not just on "how easily that knowledge can be transported, interpreted, and absorbed" (Simonin 1999, p.597) but also on the ability of the client to gather relevant and accurate knowledge internally and to make it available to the provider. Our results should encourage scholars to explore in more depth the inter-organizational impacts of factors grounded within the client's organization. For example, the quality of inter-organizational communication might be significantly affected by the structure of the communication channels employed in inter-organizational knowledge transfer. Whether employees from the business domain communicate directly with the vendor or through a liaison unit which filters and consolidates the information transfer between client and IT provider might affect, for example, the ambiguity of the transferred knowledge. Moreover, client-internal IT management processes, the communication and interaction structures between different domains, the flexibility of client's IT architecture, and the composition of the retained organization or liaison unit are just a few factors that may have a major impact on the outcomes of inter-organizational cooperation with outsourcing vendors. Investigating these potential impact factors would shift the focus of research towards the client's preparedness for successful outsourcing, which up to now has received only minor academic attention.

The insight that internal IT business alignment had a significant impact on the client-provider relationship and on the outcomes of outsourcing contains a direct implication for practice. When contemplating outsourcing as an option for IT governance, managers should not only focus their attention on factors like contractual issues and finding a suitable provider, but also on their own internal alignment – on their ability to aggregate and integrate information from different stakeholders within the firm and to make it available in an appropriate form to the provider. Firm-internal inter-domain communication and interaction should be fostered in order to strengthen the cognitive ties between employees from business and IT domains, which prove to be the main driver for effective and reliable information transfer between organizational units. This in turn should foster the client firm's ability to remove ambiguity from the knowledge which needs to be transferred to the vendor and to make available reliable and accurate information. The following table summarizes the results and the contribution of this study.

Research Question	Results	Theoretical contribution	Practical contribution
What is the impact of client's inner-organizational IT-business alignment on the inter-organizational relationship with the outsourcing vendor?	Inner-organizational alignment strongly impacts inter-organizational communication quality and service quality by allowing the client to aggregate and deliver relevant information about the own specifics to the IT provider. Moreover, internal alignment allows the client to formulate change requests more precisely and accurately, which fosters the provider's ability to implement changes more timely and reliably. However, in time, this impact becomes weaker, as the provider acquires more knowledge about its client's particularities.	The effectiveness of knowledge transfer in outsourcing relationships depends not just on its transferability and on provider's absorptive capacity, but also on client's ability to gather accurate and relevant information internally and to make it available to the provider.	Besides focusing on contractual issues, finding suitable providers, and on relationship management issues, managers should also focus on the own organizational readiness to aggregate and provide relevant information to the provider.

Table 6: Summary of Results

8 Conclusion

The objective of this study was to assess the impact of client-internal alignment and communication quality on the quality of the relationship with external IT providers (as reflected by the client-provider communication quality), and on the provider's service quality (as reflected by the two SERVQUAL (Parasuraman et al. 1988) dimensions "reliability" and "responsiveness"). In addition to confirming the widely-spread belief that knowledge sharing between client and provider by means of qualitative communication was an important predictor for outsourcing success, we could also demonstrate a clear *inter-organizational impact of client's inner-organizational communication and alignment*. Complementing works which have examined factors outside the client's organizational context – like, e.g., the role of contract completeness and the importance of choosing a suitable vendor – we were able to empirically show that the *client-internal organizational context* played a considerable role for establishing qualitative relationships with IT providers and for achieving benefits from outsourcing.

9 References

Alavi, M., and Leidner, D.E. "Review: Knowledge Management and Knowledge Management Systems: Conceptual Foundations and Research Issues," *MIS Quarterly* (25:1) 2001, pp 107-136.

Alborz, S., Seddon, P.B., and Scheepers, R. "Impact of configuration on IT outsourcing relationships," Americas Conference on Information Systems, New York, 2004.

Athanassiou, N., and Nigh, D. "Internationalization, tacit knowledge and the top management teams of MNCs," *Journal of International Business Studies* (31:3) 2000, pp 471-487.

Bassellier, G. "Information Technology Competence of Business Managers: A Definition and Research Model," *Journal of Management Information Systems* (17:4) 2001, pp 159-182.

Bassellier, G., and Benbasat, I. "Business Competence of Information Technology Professionals: Conceptual Development and Influence on IT-Business Partnerships," *MIS Quarterly* (28:4) 2004, pp 673-694.

Bassellier, G., Benbasat, I., and Reich, B.H. "The Influence of Business Managers' IT Competence on Championing IT," *Information Systems Research* (14:4) 2003, pp 317-336.

Beimborn, D., Franke, J., Wagner, H.-T., and Weitzel, T. "The Impact of Outsourcing on IT Business Alignment and IT Flexibility: A Survey in the German Banking Industry," 12th Americas Conference on Information Systems (AMCIS 2006), Acapulco, Mexico, 2006.

Beimborn, D., Franke, J., Wagner, H.-T., and Weitzel, T. "The Impact of Operational Alignment on IT Flexibility - Empirical Evidence from a Survey in the German Banking Industry," 13th Americas Conference on Information Systems (AMCIS 2007), Keystone (CO), USA, 2007.

Bergeron, F., Raymond, L., and Rivard, S. "Ideal patterns of strategic alignment and business performance," *Information & Management* (41:8) 2004, pp 1003-1020.

Blumenberg, S. "IT Outsourcing Relationship Quality Dimensions and Drivers: Empirical Evidence from the Financial Industry " Proceedings of the 14th Americas Conference on Information Systems (AMCIS), Toronto, Canada, 2008.

Blumenberg, S., Beimborn, D., and König, W. "Determinants of IT Outsourcing Relationships: A Conceptual Model," Proceedings of the 41st Annual Hawaii International Conference on System Sciences (HICSS-41), Waikoloa, HI, USA, 2008.

Chan, Y.E., Huff, S.L., Barclay, D.W., and Copeland, D.G. "Business Strategic Orientation, Information Systems Strategic Orientation, and Strategic Alignment," *Information Systems Research* (8:2) 1997, pp 125-150.

Chan, Y.E., and Reich, B.H. "IT alignment: what have we learned?," *Journal of Information Technology* (22:4), September 2007, pp 297-315.

Chiasson, M.W., and Davidson, E. "Taking Industry Seriously in Information Systems Research," *MIS Quarterly* (29:4) 2005, pp 591-605.

Cragg, P., King, M., and Hussin, H. "IT alignment and firm performance in small manufacturing firms," *Journal of Strategic Information Systems* (11:2) 2002, pp 109-132.

Currie, W.L. "A knowledge-based risk assessment framework for evaluating web-enabled application outsourcing projects," *International Journal of Project Management* (21:3) 2003, pp 207-217.

Dibbern, J., Winkler, J., and Heinzl, A. "Explaining Variations in Client Extra Costs between Software Projects Offshored to India," *MIS Quarterly* (32:2) 2008, pp 333-366.

Feurer, R., Chaharbaghi, K., Weber, M., and Wargin, J. "Aligning Strategies, Processes, and IT: A Case Study," *Information Systems Management* (17:1) 2000, pp 23-34.

Goles, T. "Vendor capabilities and outsourcing success: A resource-based view," *Wirtschaftsinformatik* (45:2) 2003, pp 199-206.

Goles, T., and Chin, W.W. "Information Systems Outsourcing Relationship Factors: Detailed Conceptualization and Initial Evidence," *The DATA BASE for Advances in Information Systems* (36:4) 2005, pp 47-67.

Gopal, A., Bostrom, R.P., and Chin, W.W. "Applying Adaptive Structuration Theory to Investigate the Process of Group Support Systems Use," *Journal of Management Information Systems* (9:3) 1993, pp 45-69.

Gordon, J.R., and Gordon, S.R. "Structuring the Interaction between IT and Business Units: Prototypes for Service Delivery," *Information Systems Management* (17:1) 2000, pp 7-16.

Grant, R.M. "Toward a knowledge-based theory of the firm," *Strategic Management Journal* (17:10) 1996, pp 109-122.

Kearns, G.S., and Lederer, A.L. "The impact of industry contextual factors on IT focus and the use of IT for competitive Advantage," *Information & Management* (41:7) 2004, pp 899-919.

Kearns, G.S., and Sabherwal, R. "Strategic Alignment Between Business and Information Technology: A Knowledge-Based View of Behaviors, Outcome, and Consequences," *Journal of Management Information Systems* (23:3) 2007, pp 129-162.

Kettinger, W.J., and Lee, C.C. "Pragmatic Perspectives on the Measurement of Information Systems Service Quality," *MIS Quarterly* (21:2) 1997, pp 223-240.

Kogut, B., and Zander, U. "Knowledge of the Firm, Combinative Capabilities, and the Replication of Technology," *Organization Science* (3:3) 1992, pp 383-397.

Lee, J.-N., and Kim, Y.-G. "Effect of partnership quality on IS outsourcing success: conceptual framework and empirical validation," *Journal of Management Information Systems* (15:4) 1999, pp 29-61.

Lee, J.N. "The impact of knowledge sharing, organizational capability and partnership quality on IS outsourcing success," *Information & Management* (38:5) 2001, pp 323-335.

Levina, N., and Ross, J.W. "From the Vendor's Perspective: Exploring the Value Proposition in IT Outsourcing," *MIS Quarterly* (27:3) 2003, pp 331-364.

Liang, H., Saraf, N., Hu, Q., and Xue, Y. "Assimilation of Enterprise Systems: The Effect of Institutional Pressures and the Mediating Role of Top Management," *MIS Quarterly* (31:1) 2007, pp 59-87.

Liebeskind, J.P. "Knowledge, Strategy, and the Theory of the Firm," *Strategic Management Journal* (17:Special Issue: Knowledge and the Firm) 1996, pp 93-107.

Lind, M.R., and Zmud, R.W. "The Influence of a Convergence in Understanding between Technology Providers and Users on Information Technology Innovativeness," *Organization Science* (2:2) 1991, pp 195-217.

Lindell, M., and Whitney, D. "Accounting for Common Method Variance in Cross-Sectional Research Designs," *Journal of Applied Psychology* (86:1) 2001, pp 114-121.

Luftman, J., and McLean, E.R. "Key issues for IT executives," *MIS Quarterly Executive* (3:2) 2004, pp 89-104.

Mao, J.-Y., Lee, J.-N., and Deng, C.-P. "Vendors' perspectives on trust and control in offshore information systems outsourcing," *Information & Management* (45:7) 2008, pp 482-492.

Martin, S., Wagner, H.-T., and Beimborn, D. "Process Documentation, Operational Alignment, and Flexibility in IT Outsourcing Relationships: A Knowledge-Based Perspective," International Conference on Information Systems (ICIS), Paris, France, 2008.

Mohr, J., and Spekman, R. "Characteristics of Partnership Success: Partnership Attributes, Communication Behavior, and Conflict Resolution Techniques," *Strategic Management Journal* (15:2) 1994, pp 135-152.

Nelson, K.M., and Cooprider, J.G. "The Contribution of Shared Knowledge to IS Group Performance," *MIS Quarterly* (20:4) 1996, pp 409-432.

Norman, P.M. "Knowledge acquisition, knowledge loss, and satisfaction in high technology alliances," *Journal of Business Research* (57:6) 2004, pp 610-619.

Parasuraman, A., Zeithaml, V.A., and Berry, L.L. "SERVQUAL: A Multiple-Item Scale for Measuring Consumer Perceptions of Service Quality," in: *Journal of Retailing*, 1988, pp. 12-40.

Penrose, E.T. *The theory of the growth of the firm* Wiley, New York, 1959.

Podsakoff, P.M., MacKenzie, S.B., Lee, J.-Y., and Podsakoff, N.P. "Common Method Bias in Behavioral Research: A Critical Review of the Literature and Recommended Remedies," *Journal of Applied Psychology* (88:5) 2003, pp 879-903.

Ranganathan, C., and Balaji, S. "Critical Capabilities for Offshore Outsourcing of Information Systems," *MIS Quarterly Executive* (6:3), September 2007, pp 147-164.

Reich, B.H., and Benbasat, I. "Measuring the Linkage Between Business and Information Technology Objectives," *MIS Quarterly* (20:1) 1996, pp 55-81.

Reich, B.H., and Benbasat, I. "Factors That Influence the Social Dimension of Alignment between Business and Information Technology Objectives," *MIS Quarterly* (24:1) 2000, pp 81-113.

Ringle, C.M., Wende, S., and Will, A. *SmartPLS 2.0 (beta)* University of Hamburg, Hamburg, 2005.

Ross, J.W., Beath, C.M., and Goodhue, D.L. "Develop Long-Term Competitiveness through IT Assets," *Sloan Management Review* (38:1) 1996, pp 31-42.

Simonin, B.L. "Ambiguity and the Process of Knowledge Transfer in Strategic Alliances," *Strategic Management Journal* (20:7), July 1999, pp 595-623.

Tallon, P.P., and Kraemer, K.L. "Fact or Fiction? A Sensemaking Perspective on the Reality Behind Executives' Perceptions of IT Business Value," *Journal of Management Information Systems* (24:1) 2007, pp 13-54.

Tan, F.B., and Gallupe, R.B. "Aligning Business and Information Systems Thinking: A Cognitive Approach," *IEEE Transactions on Engineering Management* (53:2) 2006, pp 223-237.

Tiwana, A. "Knowledge Partitioning in Outsourced Software Development: A Field Study," International Conference on Information Systems (ICIS), Seattle, Washington, 2003.

Tiwana, A., Bharadwaj, A., and Sambamurthy, V. "The antecedents of information systems development capability in firms: a knowledge integration perspective," Proceedings of the Twenty-Fourth International Conference in Information Systems, Seattle, Washington, USA, 2003, pp. 246-258.

Wagner, H.-T. *A Resource-based Perspective on IT Business Alignment and Firm Performance: Theoretical foundation and empirical evidence* ibidem-Verlag, Stuttgart, 2007.

Worren, N., Moore, K., and Cardona, P. "Modularity, Strategic Flexibility, and Firm Performance: A Study of the Home Appliance Industry," *Strategic Management Journal* (23:12) 2002, pp 1123-1140.

10 Appendix

Factor	Group with relationship of 5 years or less				Group with relationship older than 5 years			
	AVE	Composite Reliability	R Square	Cronbach's Alpha	AVE	Composite Reliability	R Square	Cronbach's Alpha
CICQ	.860	.924	.516	.837	.788	.881	.480	.732
CPCQ	.784	.916	.240	.865	.736	.893	.017	.820
REL	.651	.848	.195	.741	.535	.767	.139	.630
RES	.623	.832	.260	.705	.630	.834	.388	.707

Table 7: Comparison of Quality Criteria for the Sub-Samples (Grouping break point set at 5 years)

Factor	Group with relationship of 5 years or less				Group with relationship of more than 5 years			
	CICQ	CPCQ	REL	RES	CICQ	CPCQ	REL	RES
CICQ	.927				.888			
CPCQ	.490	.885			.131	.858		
REL	.405	.353	.807		-.085	.349	.731	
RES	.419	.459	.554	.790	.032	.621	.566	.794

Table 8: Correlations of Latent Variables and AVE Square Root (Shaded Cells) in the Sub-Samples (Grouping break point set at 5 years)

Factor	Group with relationship of 10 years or less				Group with relationship older than 10 years			
	AVE	Composite Reliability	R Square	Cronbach's Alpha	AVE	Composite Reliability	R Square	Cronbach's Alpha
CICQ	.850	.919	.538	.824	.780	.876	.433	.718
CPCQ	.763	.906	.160	.848	.745	.897	.011	.829
REL	.621	.830	.174	.707	.540	.772	.174	.637
RES	.617	.829	.260	.691	.645	.844	.377	.722

Table 9: Comparison of Quality Criteria for the Sub-Samples (Grouping break point set at 10 years)

Factor	Group with relationship of 10 years or less				Group with relationship of more than 10 years			
	CICQ	CPCQ	REL	RES	CICQ	CPCQ	REL	RES
CICQ	.922				.883			
CPCQ	.400	.873			.103	.863		
REL	.371	.324	.788		-.168	.362	.735	
RES	.321	.492	.553	.786	.019	.613	.565	.803

Table 10: Correlations of Latent Variables and AVE Square Root (Shaded Cells) in the Sub-Samples (Grouping break point set at 10 years)

***ibidem*-**Verlag

Melchiorstr. 15

D-70439 Stuttgart

info@ibidem-verlag.de

www.ibidem-verlag.de
www.ibidem.eu
www.edition-noema.de
www.autorenbetreuung.de